Texas Panhandle
T A L E S

Texas Panhandle
TALES

Mike Cox

Charleston · London

THE
History
PRESS

Published by The History Press
Charleston, SC 29403
www.historypress.net

Copyright © 2012 by Mike Cox
All rights reserved

First published 2012

Manufactured in the United States

ISBN 978.1.60949.611.1

Library of Congress CIP data applied for.

CONTENTS

Introduction 9

INDIANS
Kate Polly's Pancakes 11
The Great Panhandle Indian Raid 14

BUFFALO HUNTERS
Zulu Stockade, Texas 18
Andrew Johnson at Adobe Walls 20
J. Wright Mooar's Buffalo 24

SOLDIERS
Our Indian Summer in the Far West 28

COWBOYS
The Pitchfork Kid 33
Panhandle Cowboy Buys Himself a Circus 36
Old XIT Hands Whoop It Up in Dalhart 38

CRITTERS
Remembering Blackie 42
The Last Buffalo 44
Antelope Still Home on the Range in the Panhandle 46

CONTENTS

LAW AND DISORDER

Dead Duck Triggers a Gun Battle 49

R.G. Miller's Big Day Was His Last 54

Clarendon's "Cowardly" Constable 55

Clairemont and Its Old Jail 58

"Kid" Murray 60

MYSTERIES

Palo Duro Mystery Man 63

Lubbock's Memphis Man and Other Spooks 67

THE WIND

Wind Wagons 71

Racing the Wind 73

Dusters 76

World's Tallest Windmill No More 79

GHOST TOWNS

Tee Pee City 83

A Letter from Estacado 85

MORE THAN NAMES ON THE MAP

Booker 88

Punkin Center 90

Earth 92

Kent County 95

CHARACTERS

Mobeetie's Parson Brown 97

Plains Pioneer Charlie Saigling 99

Panhandle Lawmaker Envisioned High Plains Statehood 102

Indian Jim 105

Gene Autry Comes to Childress 108

Contents

Laughing Matters

Brownfield's Roosevelt Riot 111

Lamesa: Home of the Chicken-Fried Steak…Not! 113

One Famous Son of Fritch 116

High Plains Ingenuity

Bone Roads 119

Cow Patties 120

Low Tech v. High Tech in the 1890s 122

Travel Trailers Panhandle Style 124

When Coins Fell from the Sky 126

Getting There and Back

Lonnie Houston's Last Ride 130

The Amarillo "Symphony" 133

Amarillo's First Airmail 136

Long Road to Hamblen Drive 138

About the Author 143

INTRODUCTION

I've been fascinated with the history of the Texas Panhandle since the summer of 1961, when my dad took me to Mobeetie in that region's northeastern corner to visit the site of old Fort Elliott.

Earlier that year, my seventh-grade Texas history teacher had all her students pick a topic on the state's history and prepare a notebook on it as a semester project. I had chosen old Texas forts. The notebook was completed and earned me an A-plus, but putting it together hooked me on the topic. That's why I talked my dad into taking me from Amarillo to Wheeler County to see where Fort Elliott had been.

The landowner and his wife graciously let us climb through the barbed-wire fence behind the roadside state historical marker near the site so we could walk around where the cavalry post had stood during its fifteen years of existence. I found a shoebox full of artifacts, including an old rifle cartridge, horseshoe nails, pieces of broken bottles and even the leather sole of an old boot I imagined had been worn by a cavalry trooper.

Also that summer, my dad let me ride the bus from Amarillo to Canyon to visit the Panhandle Plains Historical Museum. Not only did I go through all the exhibits, but I also spent time in the museum archive, reading up on Fort Elliott.

I was just a teenager then, but my interest in history has lasted, while my youth has not.

This book, the third in a series based on my weekly "Texas Tales" newspaper column, includes forty-six pieces focusing on the interesting people, places and history of the top of Texas, that straight-lined, near-square part of the state that early on struck someone as the "handle" of the "pan" that constitutes the rest of the Lone Star State.

Most descriptions of the Panhandle say it includes twenty-six counties, bordered on the south by Parmer, Castro, Swisher, Briscoe, Hall and Childress. That area covers 25,823.9 square miles, almost 10 percent of Texas. Nearly a half million people live there, but with that much land, there is still plenty of wide-open space, from the rich grasslands of Dallam County in the northwest corner to the awesome grandeur of Palo Duro Canyon to the south. The "capital" of the Panhandle is Amarillo, bisected by Interstate 40, the old Route 66. For this book, I have included some stories from the South Plains, as well as the Panhandle proper, but culturally and topographically, there's not much difference between the two regions except altitude above sea level.

It's too complicated a story to tell here, but while I was born in Amarillo (where my dad was a longtime newspaperman), I grew up "down state," as they say in the Panhandle. Even so, since half my family lived there, I visited Amarillo regularly and still return every chance I get.

My dad, my grandmother and other immediate family members who lived in Amarillo are all gone, but the high, vast landscape, the deep canyons and all the stories they hold endure.

INDIANS

KATE POLLY'S PANCAKES

Next time you fry a stack of pancakes, imagine what it would be like if your life and the well-being of your children depended on it.

In the spring of 1874, Kate Polly and her husband, Ephraim, lived with their young daughters, two-year-old Katie and four-year-old Annie, in a dugout at the headwaters of Morgan Creek in what is now Hemphill County. They had been among the first Anglo families to settle on the High Plains. Back then, the Panhandle had yet to see a plow, its sweeping, treeless plains covered in luxuriant native grasses and vast herds of buffalo and antelope. A person could see for miles in any direction.

And one morning early that summer, bad trouble loomed on the horizon.

Home alone with her children, Kate busied herself with the daily chores. Her husband, who had been a hospital steward in the army, had left to tend to a sick buffalo hunter and then gather forage to sell to the military at Camp Supply in Indian Territory (now Oklahoma). At some point, Kate happened to look outside and saw something not everyone lived to describe: hundreds of Indians on horseback, all armed with either bows or rifles, quietly encircling their dugout.

With gestures underscored by bruising pinches, the Indians' headman communicated that he and the other Indians wanted food. Sizing up their number, Kate decided the easiest meal would be pancakes. After lighting a fire in her wood-burning stove, she donned her apron and started mixing batter. Whenever Kate had to stop and mix more batter, the next Indian in line would pinch her and motion for her to start cooking again.

A lone Plains Indian surveys the vast Panhandle landscape in this 1907 painting. *Author's collection.*

One by one, the warriors filed through the Polly home, grabbing handfuls of steaming pancakes straight off the top of the hot stove and wolfing them down with great delight. (The Indians apparently did not need melted butter and maple syrup to enhance their enjoyment of Kate's hotcakes.)

Finally, near sundown, the family's 192-pound flour barrel ran empty. Exhausted, Kate picked up her youngest child and walked slowly outside, plopping down on a cottonwood log. Oblivious to the watching Indians, she opened her blouse and began nursing her daughter.

Seeing that their meal service had stopped, several of the Indians came up and pinched her again, pointing toward their stomachs and the dugout. They wanted more pancakes.

Dead tired, Kate shook her head and ran her finger across her throat in a universally understood gesture. She had been standing over a hot stove all

This watercolor by Charles M. Russell depicts Plains Indian holding a scalp. *Author's collection.*

day long, flipping hotcakes for hundreds of hostile Indians. If they wanted to kill her now, fine. At least she wouldn't have to wash the dishes.

Impressed by her pluck, as well as her cooking, the Indians mounted their horses, rounded up the Polly family's milk cows and rode off through a canyon to the northwest. The cows later wandered back, but not the Indians.

From Morgan Creek, the war party rode on to a buffalo hunter's camp at a place called Adobe Walls in what is now Hutchinson County. At dawn on June 27, the Indians attacked. Aided by Billy Dixon's famous near-mile-long shot that toppled the Indians' medicine man from his horse, the buffalo hunters managed to hold off the warriors, and all but two of the defenders lived to tell about it. The incident triggered the Red River War, the last stand of the Plains Indians in the Panhandle.

When Ephraim returned from his trip, he found the dugout surrounded by unshod pony tracks and estimated that as many as seven hundred Indians had descended on the place in his absence. He reckoned them to have been a mix of Comanche, Kiowa and Cheyenne.

When the U.S. cavalry marched into the Panhandle to deal with the hostile Indians, the Pollys moved back to Fort Hays in Kansas, which is where they had come from. They returned to Texas at the end of the war in 1876 and operated a stagecoach stop on Commission Creek (in present Lipscomb County, south of what would become Higgins) along the road from Dodge City, Kansas, to newly established Fort Elliott near Mobeetie in

Wheeler County. The Pollys stayed there until 1885, when they returned to Hemphill County. When that county was organized two years later, Ephraim got elected as the first county judge.

Hemphill County is where the couple stayed for the rest of their lives. Kate died at fifty-seven on May 2, 1899, and was buried in Canadian. Her husband joined her in the same cemetery after his death on April 21, 1905. He had made it to sixty-three.

Fortunately, the story of Kate's 1874 pancake dinner did not die with the pioneer couple. Kate's oldest daughter, by then Mrs. D.M. Hargrave, had been just old enough to remember the incident and passed the tale on to her daughter, the future Mrs. E.R. Cloyd. Mrs. Cloyd, in turn, put the story on paper for inclusion in a history of Lipscomb County published in 1976.

Whether Kate Polly could ever stomach cooking pancakes again is not recorded, but given her grit, she probably did. After all, flapjacks saved her scalp and probably averted a life of captivity for her children.

THE GREAT PANHANDLE INDIAN RAID

Destined to gain a national reputation as a fearless Texas Ranger captain, when William Jesse McDonald arrived in the Panhandle in the winter of 1891, he expected to stay busy as a law enforcement officer in a still sparsely settled section of the state. But he sure didn't anticipate what happened on the night of January 29 that year.

As a teenager, McDonald had come to East Texas from Mississippi after the Civil War. Having studied business at a commercial college in New Orleans, he evolved from merchant to lawman, serving as a deputy sheriff, special ranger and deputy U.S. marshal. By the mid-1880s, he had moved to Hardeman County in northwest Texas.

A skinny six-footer as tough as a tar-soaked telegraph pole, McDonald soon established a reputation for effectiveness as a peace officer, but his long-standing friendship with the newly elected governor, Jim Hogg, is what got him appointed as captain of Company B when S.A. McMurray left the force. McDonald assumed command of the company in Amarillo, a fairly new railroad town on the High Plains.

Arriving on the Fort Worth and Denver Railroad about midnight on January 29, 1891, McDonald found a hotel and went to bed as soon as he could. He had just drifted off when someone banged on his door with an urgent wire: Indians had raided Hall County, about one hundred miles to the

An array of Comanche Indians after they were relegated to a reservation. *Author's collection.*

west. His blue eyes smiling, the new captain read the telegram and laughed, assuming some of the rangers in his company had decided to welcome him into state service with a practical joke. It had been a decade since any hostile Indians had caused problems in Texas.

McDonald went back to sleep. But soon, other telegrams came, including a dire-sounding message from the railroad superintendent. Still not believing that Indians had dared leave their reservation in Indian Territory, McDonald nevertheless realized he had to investigate. The new captain dressed and walked to the telegraph office for more information. After an exchange of messages with the operator in Salisbury, who ended his last transmission with "Good-bye, I'm going now myself," McDonald got the railroad to put together a special train for an emergency trip to Hall County.

At virtually every point in the Panhandle that had telegraph service, word sparked across the wire that Comanche and Kiowa Indians were spilling into Texas from their reservations in Indian Territory. People's reactions ranged from pure panic to expressions of bravado from young cowboys eager to prove their mettle in an Indian fight.

In Armstrong County south of Claude, Virginia Hamblen happened to look out her kitchen window toward the nearby Luttrell place. Seeing her friend Molly Luttrell frantically chasing a horse around their yard, Mrs. Hamblen knew something unusual was afoot. As she continued to watch, she saw Molly finally catch the horse and swing up on its back. Once in the

A group of rowdy cowboys led to the Great Indian Raid, but these High Plains waddies preferred a game of low-stakes poker. *XIT Ranch Musuem, Dalhart, Texas.*

saddle, the housewife started galloping across the prairie in the direction of the Hamblen residence.

"Molly, what in the world is the matter?"

"The Indians are coming!" she cried.

"What do you mean?" Virginia asked.

"The Indians are coming. They are tearing up the railroad track, killing women and children and burning houses! What are we going to do?"

As soon as both families got everyone rounded up and threw their essential belongings in wagons, they left for the more easily defended dugout of another nearby family. When they got there, they found other families had the same idea. With the women and children huddled in the dugout, the men circled their wagons around it and took positions with rifles at the ready to await developments.

During the night, every coyote yelp and owl hoot sent adrenaline surging since all knew that Indians communicated with animal sounds. On top of that, one of the women was pregnant and anticipated going into labor at any moment. Another child had the croup and had to be dosed with sugar and coal oil all night. Only the youngest of the children got any sleep.

The Palo Duro Hotel in Washburn filled with terrified area residents rushing to town on the theory that there would be safety in numbers. They selected a nearby cellar as a refuge of last resort. Intent on saving their families, some men hurried their wives and children to the depot to board the westbound train for Denver while they faced the Indians. Volunteer scouts saddled up to look for any sign of the approaching war party, while men—and some women—armed with Winchesters patrolled the streets.

When McDonald and his rangers arrived in Salisbury, the town looked abandoned, its populace in hiding. But rifle barrels bristled from practically every window. The rangers loaded their horses off the train, saddled up and rode east from town to look for any signs of the carnage that had been reported. All they found was that the country lay as devoid of Indians as settlers.

It did not take the captain long to discover the source of the reported Indian outbreak: a tenderfoot had panicked at the sight of a bunch of liquored-up cowboys raising Cain around their campfire. Even so, reports of killing and scalping had swept across the Panhandle like a prairie fire. The *Canyon City Echo* even reported that "state rangers were fighting the Indians and that two or three of the rangers had been killed."

In reality, the only loss the rangers suffered was sleep. Failing to see the humor of the situation, McDonald disgustedly returned to Amarillo to get some rest.

The new ranger captain may have never known that the Indian scare actually led to at least one death in the Panhandle. As young Virgil Rice of Washburn rode home with his brothers after it had been positively established that no Indian raid had occurred, he decided to demonstrate just how well he would have handled things if renegades had really attacked. Pulling his pistol with impressive speed, he intended to impress his younger brothers by letting go a round as if shooting an attacking Indian. Unfortunately, Rice proved a little too quick on the trigger, and the bullet killed his horse.

Buffalo Hunters

Zulu Stockade, Texas

Despite their genteel upbringing in England, enjoying a white Christmas probably was the last thing on the minds of the two young buffalo hunters when the snow started falling.

They were hunting on Christmas Day 1873 in a break along North Palo Duro Creek in what would become Hansford County when a gentle snow grew into a dangerous blizzard. Realizing they faced a long winter, they built themselves a dugout with cottonwood timber and buffalo hides and settled in until the weather broke.

Freezing precipitation did not constitute the only danger that winter. The Comanche and Kiowa still considered the High Plains of Texas their hunting ground, but brothers Jim and Bob Cator managed to keep their scalps until the U.S. cavalry drove the Indians out of the Panhandle during the Red River War of 1874–75.

The Cator boys had come to the United States from England in 1871 and quickly headed west from New York. Working their way through Kansas, they came to Dodge City and decided to take up buffalo hunting. In sixty days during the summer of 1873, they killed nearly seven thousand buffalo, mostly in Kansas. But in following the herd, they drifted into the Panhandle like the shaggy animal they unintentionally did their part to make extinct. When the market value of the hides dropped for a time, they took to killing gray wolves and coyotes for the bounty, an enterprise they called "wolfing."

Though the Cators had moved on from their dugout in future Hansford County after the weather began warming up, they liked the country they

Zulu Stockade was a stop on the well-used trail from Dodge City, Kansas, to Tascosa. *Photo by Mike Cox.*

had seen. Five years later, they came back and stayed, soon furnishing the Panhandle with one of its most evocative place names.

Not far from where they had wintered in their dugout in 1873, the Cators—again using native cottonwood—built a three-room picket house that served as both a residence and stagecoach stop between the area's two principal communities, Dodge City and Tascosa, a distance of 242 miles. From Tascosa, the trail continued on to Fort Bascom in New Mexico Territory.

The buffalo just about killed out, the Cators began running a store to capitalize on the traffic along the road. The brothers merely wanted to make a living, but their combination residence, stage stand and retail establishment would come to be regarded as the first structure built by Anglos in the Panhandle north of the Canadian River.

By December 1880, the area had gotten so civilized that the Cators applied for a post office. An obvious element of the process involved coming up with a name for their community. What they decided on turned out to be one of the most un-Texany-sounding names in the Panhandle: Zulu Stockade.

The bloody Zulu War had just ended in Africa, and that had been a subject in the correspondence between the brothers and their parents, who referred to the Lone Star State as "Darkest Texas," a play on "Darkest Africa." As far as they and their sons were concerned, the Panhandle lay as wild and untamed as the Kingdom of Zululand. Of course, no Zulus could be found within thousands of miles of Zulu Stockade. And the newly named Panhandle settlement lacked a stockade as well, tall timber being in pretty short supply on the plains.

In 1886, newly married Jim Cator built a substantial rock house on the ranch land he had purchased about twenty miles from Hansford, then the county seat. Meanwhile, the exotically named trading post and stage stop continued to do well until railroads supplanted most travel by horse-drawn coach in the late 1880s. However, Zulu Stockade hung on as a rural post office until the early 1900s.

Though that colorful place name in time faded from the map, the Cators not only stayed around, but more of them came to Texas. First to arrive was a sister, Clara; then a younger brother, Bert; and finally another brother, Leslie. That brother brought along his new bride, Bessie Donelson.

Jim Cator, because he had a son with the same name, eventually became known as "Old Jim" Cator. He served as Hansford County's first judge and its second sheriff, living on until the fall of 1927.

Bert Cator also served two terms as sheriff, from 1893 to 1895 and again from 1900 to 1909. Born in a dugout in 1902, Cator's son Marshall went on to become one of the Panhandle's most prominent cattlemen. Two years before his death at the age of ninety-nine in 2002, he received the prestigious Chester A. Reynolds Memorial Award from the National Cowboy Hall of Fame and Western Heritage Center in Oklahoma City.

By the time Marshall Cator came along, the county had its first newspaper, the *Hansford Investigator*. The editor of that sheet, in discussing the fortitude it took to do business in a relatively new area, said: "The Palo Duro valley of the Panhandle country is a household word, and it has been made possible only by those who are what may be termed 'nerve' enough to penetrate this beautiful section of the Lord's domain."

The Cator clan did not lack in nerve or verve.

Andrew Johnson at Adobe Walls

Fifty years earlier to the day, waking up to find themselves surrounded by hundreds of hostile Indians, Andrew Johnson and the other occupants of the Panhandle trading post and buffalo hunter's camp called Adobe Walls had fought desperately for their lives. Now an old man, Johnson stood facing a crowd of more than two thousand, a different kind of fear twisting his gut.

One of only two living survivors of that July 27, 1874 battle, he had been invited to talk about what he had seen on this very spot a half century before. The occasion was the dedication of a large granite monument commemorating the fight that led to what came to be called the Red River War, the U.S. military campaign that vanquished the Plains Indian from Texas after fifty years of vicious conflict.

In the summer of 1924, Johnson's final journey to Adobe Walls started where the first one had begun so many years before—in Dodge City, Kansas.

A Swedish immigrant born in 1845, Johnson had come to Dodge City in the spring of 1874 and opened Western Kansas's first blacksmith shop. He ran the business only a few months before selling out to Adam Schmidt after deciding he could earn a better, if more dangerous, living hunting buffalo in Texas. That marked the start of a lifelong friendship with the Schmidt family, which is why in the spring or early summer of 1924, Johnson came to Adam's son Heinrich to ask a favor. Heinrich Schmidt, better known in town as "Heinie," had served as Dodge City's postmaster and edited the *Daily Globe*.

Artist's conception of Indians attacking Adobe Walls. *Author's collection.*

In his prime, Johnson could shoe a horse, skin a buffalo, grade tanned hides and wrangle recalcitrant mules. And later in life, he had made a good hand running a cement crew replacing Dodge City's old wooden sidewalks with smooth pavement, branding each segment "AJ." But he knew nothing of writing a speech. Accordingly, he approached Schmidt to type up something he could read when the big day came.

As soon as was convenient, Schmidt called on Johnson at his two-room frame house on Front Street, just south of Dodge City's famous Boot Hill Cemetery, to interview him about his experiences at Adobe Walls.

"We used a large box of matches keeping Andy's pipe going and the lamp lighted," Schmidt later remembered. "It was 2:00 a.m. when I left his house and started for home. Andy, his feet in carpet slippers, walked with me to the courthouse corner. Finally, I asked, 'Andy, is there anything you forgot to tell me?' Putting his arms on my shoulder, he said, 'Heinie, put lots of roses in it.'"

Johnson had made the 150-mile trip many times in a wagon, but as the day of the monument dedication approached, his friend Tom Stauth offered to drive him from Dodge to the site of Adobe Walls. Joining them for the ride would be O.A. (Brick) Bond and James O'Neal.

When the Kansas men motored to within sight of where the old trading post had stood, Johnson began to get excited. Stauth hardly had time to stop his Model T before the old man bailed out, running almost child-like to the spot where he had fought to save his scalp so many years before.

Yellowfish, the last surviving Comanche who took part in the Adobe Walls fight, around 1915. *Hutchinson County Museum, Borger, Texas.*

After taking in the scene, Johnson and the other Dodge City men enjoyed a barbecue lunch hosted by W.T. Coble, whose Turkey Track Ranch took in the Adobe Walls site. Heartily supporting the monument, Coble had deeded to the Panhandle Plains Historical Society a plot of land that included the graves of the men killed in the fight.

With airplanes circling overhead, the dedication program began at 1:00 p.m. When it came time for him to step forward and make his talk, Johnson tried but couldn't do it. Having lost a battle with himself, Johnson handed the speech his younger friend Schmidt had typed up for him to Gene Howe, editor of the *Amarillo Globe-News*. Like most everyone else in Kansas, Johnson knew Howe's father, writer Ed Howe.

Not wishing to further embarrass the elderly survivor, Howe cleared his throat and started reading Johnson's narrative. After covering a little background, the history-minded newspaper editor moved into the heart of Johnson's narrative.

"On the morning of June 27, 1874, at two o'clock in the morning, the ridgepole in Hanrahan's saloon broke with such a loud noise that it woke every man in the camp," he read.

To keep the roof of the dugout from caving in, Johnson and others got on top and threw off as much dirt as they could. That didn't take long, and everyone went back to bed, including Johnson.

But fellow hunter Billy Dixon, who planned on leaving later that morning for Dodge City with a load of hides, decided he might as well stay up. His decision, and that broken ridgepole, proved providential.

"Billy…observed the Indians coming up the [Canadian] river between the high bluffs east of the battleground and the riverbed," Howe continued for Johnson. "He gave the alarm, and we immediately began preparations to ward off the attack."

What Johnson saw that morning struck him as beautiful in an awful sort of way, and he remembered it clearly to that day.

"In full war paint it was a colorful scene, one that will never again be duplicated," Howe went on. "Many of [the Indians] were armed with rifles… and revolvers; many carried bows and arrows, and many carried…lances."

After the fight began, the editor continued for Johnson, "the action for thirty or forty minutes was too brisk for anyone to describe. Each man was too busy to notice what the others were doing."

"We had several dogs and a pet coyote in camp when the fight began," Johnson recalled in his narrative. "They all ran off. The dogs came back in three or four days, but the coyote never did. I am sure that he joined the Indians."

Johnson was back in Dodge City for good by 1878, when the last shipment of forty thousand buffalo hides left town. With the buffalo nearly extinct, Johnson turned to other ways of making a living.

Despite the trouble he had talking about the battle before the large crowd that turned out for the monument dedication, it never bothered Johnson to discuss with folks one-on-one his role in the fight.

One time, Schmidt later recalled, when Johnson had walked into the newspaper office for some reason or other, he had jokingly said, "Andy, Mike Sutton told me that Bat Materson told him you crawled under the bed during the fight."

Johnson's facial expression hardened, and he abruptly turned and walked out of the office. About an hour later, Schmidt had another visitor, Mike Sutton.

"My goodness, Heinie, what did you tell Andy Johnson? He came into my office and pulled off his coat, saying he was going to whip me. He kept saying, 'It's a lie! I never crawled under the bed!'"

On June 12, 1925—less than a year after the dedication of the monument at Adobe Walls—Johnson joined his fellow defenders in death. He is buried in Dodge City's Maple Grove Cemetery.

J. Wright Mooar's Buffalo

The rifle roared, a .50-caliber hunk of lead smacked into the side of the buffalo and the huge, shaggy animal tumbled to the ground.

That scene played out all across the Texas plains during the 1870s, but this was no ordinary bison—it was all white, one of only seven albino bison known to have been killed on the North American continent. The animal was taken adjacent to Deep Creek, about ten miles north of present-day Snyder.

While buffalo no longer roam the plains, a life-sized bronze statue commemorating that white buffalo stands in the Scurry County courthouse square. Beneath the buffalo is a historical marker about J. Wright Mooar, the man who brought the white beast down.

Mooar killed the white buffalo on October 7, 1876, with a Sharps rifle he had purchased in Dodge City, Kansas. At the time, the greatest buffalo hunt—slaughter is a better word—in recorded history was in progress. Hunters killed the animals primarily for their hides, which were used for many things. The carcasses were left to rot on the plains, the bones eventually bleaching in the sun.

Said to have killed twenty-two thousand buffalo from 1870 to 1880, Mooar was born on August 10, 1851, in Vermont. He came to Texas in 1873 with his brother, John Webb Mooar. He had started his career colorlessly enough as a streetcar conductor in Chicago. He also worked as a carpenter and spent a brief time employed by the army in Kansas as a woodcutter before he became a buffalo hunter.

Mooar first began killing buffalo to supply the army with meat. When demand ran high, he could get a quarter a pound for buffalo meat. In slack times, the market dropped to a nickel a pound. In 1876, the same year he took the white buffalo, Mooar sold sixty-two thousand pounds of meat at Fort Griffin. He made only seven and a half cents a pound on that deal but netted $12,000 for all the hides.

From Fort Griffin, Mooar and four other men came to what would become Scurry County and made camp on a stream Mooar named Deep Creek. A week later, his brother and five other hunters joined them. They built a dugout, the first residence in future Scurry County.

The Indians considered the white buffalo to be sacred and would not kill one. But Mooar was not the superstitious type. Unlike many buffalo hunters, however, he was said to have respected the Plains Indians, whose existence ultimately depended on the buffalo. In fact, while most of the rough-hewn types who made their living killing buffalo would just as soon kill Indians if they got the chance, Mooar later told interviewers that he had always avoided any confrontations with the people who had the plains and the buffalo first.

The white buffalo in downtown Snyder is eight feet long and five and a half feet high at the shoulder. Though as large as some buffalo were in real life, the statue is said to be smaller than the bull Mooar killed. Mooar, of course, had skinned the real white buffalo and had its hide tanned in Dodge City. He later displayed it for a time in New York and at the St. Louis Exposition in 1904. The hide still exists in the possession of the descendants of his adopted son.

Most buffalo hunters were not noted for their placid demeanors. Operating well beyond the settlements, they enforced their own law or simply did without.

The same year Mooar killed the white buffalo, Jim, Jeff and Ben Webb moved to the Deep Creek country from downstate in Austin. They found the hunting good, but they had left their families back in Central Texas and missed them. Here's a story Mooar knew well, even if he wasn't involved.

Deciding to go fetch their kinfolk, the Webbs left the buffalo hunting grounds in the vicinity of future Snyder and skirted the Colorado River

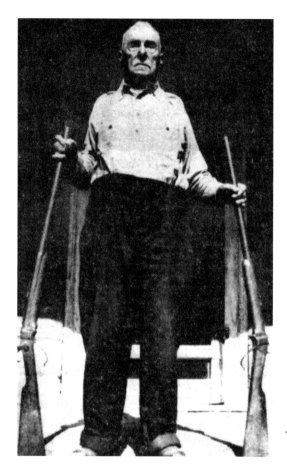

J. Wright Mooar as an old man displaying two of his old buffalo guns. *Author's collection.*

on their way down to Austin. When they returned to their camp with their families, they got a grim welcome. As they approached, they saw a body swinging in the breeze at the end of a rope tied to one of the rare trees sturdy enough to hang a man.

Nearby, a group of buffalo hunters had gotten drunk and were working on getting drunker. As the Webb boys got the story, the recently departed fellow had killed a man while arguing over cards.

The victim's friends, convening a kangaroo court, sentenced the killer to death by firing squad. But being too drunk to aim straight, they only wounded the condemned man. To put him out of his misery, they strung him up and let him strangle. Not wanting their families to be any more traumatized than they already were, the Webbs asked their colleagues to cut down the body. The hunters complied, burying him near the man he had killed.

Like those rowdy hunters, Mooar had followed the herds all over the Panhandle and South Plains, but after the buffalo had been hunted out, he decided to stay along Deep Creek. He bought land and took up ranching about ten miles northwest of Snyder.

Mooar remained a bachelor for a long time, but in 1898 at Colorado City, he married Julia Swartz. The couple never had any children, but in 1903 a fourteen-year-old boy named T.J. McDonnell hired on at Mooar's ranch. The teenager had been in ill health but soon got better. The Mooars became attached to him and eventually went to district court in Snyder to formally adopt him as their son.

After Mrs. Mooar died in 1922, Mooar continued to live on his ranch, but as he grew older, he spent more and more time at McDonnell's home in Snyder. That's where he died on May 1, 1940, at the age of eighty-nine. Though his only blood relatives were a niece and nephew in Atlanta, Georgia, and a niece in California, an estimated 3,500 people attended his funeral.

Mooar never got to enjoy the humor of it, but the first white buffalo statue in Snyder, one made of fiberglass, featured obvious-to-all male attributes. When someone carefully examined the preserved skin of the white buffalo Mooar had killed, they realized the buffalo had been female. The original statue on the courthouse square was retired, replaced by a life-sized sculpture of a female bison.

SOLDIERS

Our Indian Summer in the Far West

When the stagecoach finally rolled to a stop in Mobeetie, one of the first things that caught Englishman Samuel Nugent Townsend's eye was a troop of cavalry mustering on the Fort Elliott parade ground.

The visitor, already planning to write a book on his exploration of the American West, quickly set up his camera and photographed the assembled horse soldiers readying for a march eastward into Indian Territory, where the Comanche and Kiowa, who had once terrorized the Panhandle, now lived on reservations.

Once he finished with his picture taking, Townsend looked up Tenth Cavalry captain Nicholas Nolan, the only officer at the fort he knew. Nolan introduced the visitor to a lieutenant and his wife, who welcomed the thirty-four-year-old bachelor to share their quarters.

Townsend's stay at Fort Elliott in the fall of 1878 would be brief but not dull. In fact, for a time, it looked like civil violence might erupt in nearby Mobeetie. Townsend, a peace-loving fellow, soon felt grateful for the protection of the fort, which stood conveniently out of pistol shot from the wild and wooly town.

As Townsend later wrote in *Our Indian Summer in the Far West*, dangerous ill will had developed following the arrest of several local ranchers (he referred to them as "large estate owners") for selling tobacco to their hands at cost without having obtained a federal license. The U.S. marshal for the area filed against them in state court for the tax law violation. But the county judge, clearly sympathetic to the locals, released some of them on slight bail and dismissed the charges against others.

Indian camp near Fort Elliott. *Author's collection.*

In reaction to that, the marshal blustered and jailed the judge, the county attorney and the sheriff for obstruction of justice. After that, the marshal rearrested the ranchers.

"The greatest excitement at once was got up in the county," Townsend wrote.

The townspeople armed themselves "to the teeth," as Townsend put it, and the English visitor was sure the marshal would be lynched. Meanwhile, the army got word not to interfere in civil matters, so the garrison at Fort Elliott remained neutral.

Eventually, the hotheaded citizenry cooled off, and the ranchers paid their fines without much additional complaint. The federal charges against the local officials, if indeed ever formally lodged, went nowhere.

"The affair subsequently terminated without bloodshed," Townsend wrote, "which goes far to prove that the days of miracles have not yet ceased."

While a guest at Fort Elliott, Townsend enjoyed a prairie chicken hunt with Captain Richard I. Escridge of the Twenty-third Infantry, a Civil War veteran originally from Missouri. Venturing from the fort in the captain's light spring wagon, Townsend found the prairie "heather-looking, but…not heathery. Thin, gold, curly, buffalo grass lies amongst, and around, large tufts of red, coarse herbage, which, had it been cut in May, would have [made] some of the sweetest hay."

As the two men rolled along, their shotguns at the ready, the captain's pointer worked hard, first to the right and then to the left, but found no birds. "His spirit and ours at length began to flag."

But then the dog froze on point.

Officer's quarters and barracks at Fort Elliott. *Author's collection.*

"Whirr went the bird, bang went one of our guns, and our first prairie grouse of the season, a lovely dark brown bird, fat as a quail, and rounded as a partridge, came to earth, as dead as her late majesty, the lamented Queen Anne."

Townsend missed several shots that afternoon, and like most unsuccessful hunters, he tended to blame it on something other than his marksmanship: "Nothing, indeed, so puts out a British sportsman as the varying strength of American powders."

The gracious captain, unaware of Townsend's prejudice against American shotgun shells, gave the Englishman the remainder of his ammunition as a parting gift.

Townsend admired more than the Panhandle landscape and its bountiful hunting opportunities. In his judgment, the women he met on the High Plains were "unusually dashing equestrians, graceful dancers, good talkers, heart-breaking flirts, and as a rule enjoy the robust health which the demi-semi wildness of their surroundings fosters, and which is denied so many of Columbia's daughters."

Historical marker at the site of old Fort Elliott near Mobeetie. *Photo by Bill G. Cox.*

Equally verbose in his praise of American horse soldiers, the visitor did question the military's designation of its frontier garrisons as forts.

"These frontier posts of the United States, though termed forts, are nearly all quite incapable of being defended," he wrote. "They are really barracks, not forts; but call them by what one may, they are the most charming possible oases in the desert of civilization which surrounds them."

The American army, Townsend continued, was not "effectively larger than our metropolitan police in London." That said, he viewed the U.S. Cavalry as one of the hardest-worked fighting units in the world: "It had to be ready to quell civil disturbances, annex Canada or Cuba, furnish perpetual escorts to all distinguished persons who travel in the wilds, and uphold the honor of the stars and stripes, mentally, morally, and by display of hospitality as well."

The troops of Fort Elliott also had to ride out on short notice in pursuit of Indians who slipped off their reservation and entered their old range in Texas. Because of that, Townsend said, the soldiers seldom appeared in "full-fig"—a popular term of the day for complete fatigue dress.

"The United States soldier in his barrack, therefore, looks rather slovenly, and the officers who seldom wear any uniform except trousers, present a rather motley appearance to an eye accustomed to the rigid dress…of European armies."

While not impressed with how Fort Elliott's horse soldiers looked, Townsend definitely liked army chow.

"A regimental mess keeps up, no doubt, to desirable extent, the esprit de corps of the regiment, and has many other virtues, not the least of which is the greatest culinary comfort with a minimum of expense," he wrote.

The pith-helmeted, monocled English gentleman had much more country to cover before he could return to write his book. So that Townsend could do some exploring on his own, the post trader furnished him with a military ambulance for the remainder of his Panhandle expedition. That wagon proved just the right size for all his gear, which included a military tent, army rations, blankets, ammunition and an India-rubber bath he had carried all the way from England.

When he left Mobeetie, he wrote, "Fort Elliott is a place more pleasant to spend a month than a week."

The writer-photographer kept careful notes throughout his journey. His book was practically ready for press by the time he got back to England. Dedicated to John George Adair Esq., whose ranch Townsend also visited, the book came out in 1880.

Fort Elliott lasted another ten years before the army considered the Panhandle safe enough to get by without a military garrison.

Cowboys

The Pitchfork Kid

The Pitchfork Kid had plenty of friends, but he enjoyed his own company.

A cowboy's cowboy, the kid sat a horse well and had the reputation of being the best roper in the Panhandle. On the sprawling Matador Ranch, where he spent much of his career as a waddy, the foreman often worked him as an "outside man," someone who didn't mind saddling up and riding off by himself to hunt up a stray.

Considering the kid's background, that was fitting duty. He was something of a dogie himself.

Born in Ohio in 1873 (no one has found the day and month or place of birth), William E. Partlow became an orphan at an early age. By 1880, when census takers canvassed the small town of Chikaskia, Kansas, they listed him as living there with his maternal grandparents. Legend has two uncles in Kansas City taking him to rear, but their generous gesture didn't atone for the fact that they made their living stealing cattle. When they got caught in the act and killed, young Billy once again was on his own.

Ridge Greathouse, a professional poisoner of wolves and other range predators, found the twelve-year-old Partlow on the streets of Kansas City and learned that he wanted to be a cowboy. Greathouse had done work for D.B. Gardner, manager of the Pitchfork Ranch west of Gutherie. Knowing Gardner was in Kansas City on business, Greathouse brought the boy to him.

Luckily for young Partlow, Gardner loved children and took him back to Texas. The boy wanted to ride the range immediately, but Gardner

The Pitchfork Kid spent much of his cowboy career on the Matador Ranch. *Author's collection.*

said he was too young and wouldn't let him stray too far from the ranch headquarters. Instead, he tried to see that the boy got some book learning, but the orphan from Kansas didn't take to that very well.

The way Gardner tried to help Billy with his education was by farming him out to neighboring rancher J.T. George and his wife, a schoolteacher. She encouraged the youngster to read, but to what extent she succeeded isn't known.

After about a year with the Georges, Billy went back to the Pitchfork, finally old enough to make a hand. And soon it became evident that cowboy life suited him well. He liked the work, and he liked the grub, preferring an ample serving of onions with just about anything he ate around the chuck wagon. Somewhere along the way, given where he worked, folks started calling him the Pitchfork Kid.

The kid worked for Gardner for a few years before moving on to an even larger operation, the giant Matador Ranch in Cottle, Dickens, Floyd and Motley Counties. Beyond his skills as a cowboy, Partlow had grown up to be a well-groomed gentleman. His friends marveled that he shaved daily, even out on the range.

In 1892, a horse he'd been trying to gentle threw him against a fence. His fellow cowboys loaded their unconscious friend into a wagon and took him to ranch headquarters. From there, the ranch sent him by train to a hospital in Trinidad, Colorado. A doctor operated on his head to relieve pressure on his swollen brain, and he came to after nineteen days in a coma.

As soon as he recovered, the kid swung back in the saddle again. He stayed with the Matador until 1907, when he decided to cut out on his own. When his business venture failed, Partlow came back to the Matador, cowboy hat in hand. But the foreman, still sore that he had left the ranch in the first place, refused to rehire him.

Despite that, the mustachioed, meerschaum pipe–smoking kid enjoyed a good reputation. When longtime ranch manager Murdo McKenzie found him on the down-and-outs in the nearby town of Matador, McKenzie asked what had happened. When Partlow said the foreman wouldn't give him a job, McKenzie wrote a letter countermanding that, and the kid once again rode for the Matador.

But the dream of many cowboys is having a spread of their own. In 1917, Partlow filed on a half section of land south of Nara Visa, New Mexico, and left the Matador for the last time. Two years later, at only forty-six, he died on December 3, 1919, when he fell from a load of hay and hit his head on a rock.

As time passed, old cowboys began telling stories about the Pitchfork Kid. And one of his former pals began to wonder where he had been buried.

In 1954, seventy-year-old Fred Hale of Amarillo, who had worked with the kid on the Matador, set out to find his friend's grave. He looked all around Glenrio and Nara Visa in New Mexico, finding no one who knew where Partlow had ended up. On a hunch, Hale checked Amarillo's Llano Cemetery and discovered his friend had been buried there. Locating the plot shown in the cemetery's records (Section 43, Lot 26, in what's called the Old Cemetery), he found the grave unmarked.

Hale collected money from some of the other still-living Matador cowboys and, in 1959, had a granite marker placed over his grave. It reads:

A Cowboy
"Pitchfork Kid"
William E. Partlow
1874   1919
An Humble Man Who Achieved Greatness Through Humility and
Loyalty to His Friends
Erected in 1959 by His Friends

Carved between Partlow's year of birth and year of death is the distinctive Pitchfork brand.

PANHANDLE COWBOY BUYS HIMSELF A CIRCUS

That Texas cowboys tended to kick up their heels after a long trail drive is well documented. But one drover's experience deserves serious consideration as the lead steer of all wild cowboy tales.

In the summer of 1896, a circus arrived in Denver. That had nothing to do with Texas cowboys except that it reminded a Colorado newspaper editor of the time a circus ran out of operating capital in Pueblo. One of the show's creditors went to court and got a judgment against the owner. To satisfy the judgment, the county sheriff would auction some of the circus stock.

As preparations proceeded for the auction, a visitor from Texas was having a little better luck financially. The cattleman had driven a large herd of cattle from the Panhandle and sold the steers, as the newspaper writer recalled, "on the Arkansas [River] to John Hill."

Though the editor used the name of the buyer, he did not identify the seller from Texas by anything other than his nickname: Buzzard. The only other clue he offered, not something that would really set one Texas cattleman apart from another, was that Buzzard had a fondness for booze.

On the day of the forced sale of circus stock, Buzzard, in the vernacular of the Victorian press, was "full." Today, we would use the word "drunk."

His pocket book also full, Buzzard got caught up in the spirit of the moment and "commenced bidding on everything that was offered for sale." Buzzard's first successful purchase was a seventeen-foot-long snake. He got the reptile for a mere $500. A Texas-sized snake was exciting enough, but then a Bengal tiger caught Buzzard's eye. Through the cowboy's sheer persistence, the big cat was his for $2,000—surely a bargain at half the price.

"He bid on everything in such a reckless manner that the sheriff and the show people were in an ecstasy of delight," the editor recalled.

Next on the block was an elephant. Buzzard checked his wallet and flung himself into the spirited bidding. To his boozy delight, he came in as high bidder on the pachyderm for just $5,000.

"Buzzard paid for everything, and being troubled with an irresistible desire to treat everybody, he soon had the show people, and every one who would drink with him, as full as himself," the editor continued.

No one in Pueblo was having a better time than the owner of the circus, who not only had gotten out of debt but also, thanks to Buzzard, had more money than the whole show was worth. And Buzzard was still buying the drinks.

A Panhandle cattleman bought himself an elephant and, while he was at it, a whole circus. *Author's collection.*

Traipsing from saloon to saloon with his entourage of citizens and show people, Buzzard decided to get into show business himself. The first step, of course, would be a parade. The circus people hitched up their wagons and saddled Buzzard's elephant.

At first, Buzzard wanted to open the show by getting in the lion cage. "The circus people," the newspaper writer related, "discovering that he was an apparently inexhaustible mine of gold, whiskey and fun, were not disposed to feed him to the lions yet…and they persuaded him that the post of honor and danger was on the back of the royal elephant."

Wearing a turban and brandishing a sword, Buzzard mounted the elephant. Then he helped his wife and children on board. With the band playing "Dixie," the parade wound through Pueblo. When the procession neared the Arkansas River, the elephant charged toward the stream. The Buzzards had managed to stay astride the animal, but he had other ideas. Sucking up a trunk full of water, he sprayed the Texas family. Then he rolled over, spilling the Texans in the river.

Buzzard managed to get his family ashore, somehow even saving his sword.

"Seated on the bank," the newspaper continued, "they presented a picture to excite pity, but the spectators laughed until everybody was hoarse."

The crowd drifted off, but the Buzzards remained on the riverbank. Whether the alcohol had begun to wear off, or whether it was the immersion in the river that had a sobering effect, Buzzard's good mood evaporated a lot faster than the muddy water soaking his clothes.

"The old man suddenly developed a belligerent spirit that caused people to do their laughing at a distance," the newspaper went on. "Every time any one approached them, he would flourish his sword and swear like a pirate."

What Buzzard did with his share of the circus was not reported. And who Buzzard was remains a mystery. One thing is for sure—he was a Panhandle cowboy who knew how to have a good time.

Old XIT Hands Whoop It Up in Dalhart

In 1936, as Texas celebrated the 100th anniversary of its independence from Mexico, an old Panhandle cowboy thought it would be good to remember another era as well—the heyday of what once had been the largest ranch in the world: the XIT.

Covering three million acres and stretching nearly two hundred miles long and up to thirty miles wide from Hockley County on the south all the way north to the Oklahoma border, the ranch covered parts of ten High Plains counties. The state had conveyed the land to a group of investors in 1882 to pay for construction of a new capitol in Austin. At its height, enclosed by six thousand miles of barbed-wire fence, the ranch ran 150,000 head of cattle, had 1,500 horses and kept 150 cowboys on its payroll. One of those cowboys was A.W. (Bill) Askew.

Originally from Marble Falls in Central Texas, Askew first came to the Panhandle in 1899. Then twenty, he cowboyed on the T.S. Bugbee Ranch near Clarendon and later worked on Charles Goodnight's famed JA Ranch before hiring on with the XIT in 1900. For the next year, in addition to punching cows, he repaired and greased windmills and hauled hay and freight on three of the giant ranch's seven divisions. Like many of his contemporaries, Askew rode his experience as a cowboy into a successful business career. After completing a six-month course at Tyler Business College, he moved to Amarillo in 1904 and opened an insurance and real estate business. Despite the Great Depression, more than thirty years later he was still in business.

Likely inspired by all the hoopla attendant to the Texas centennial, and at fifty-seven well aware of time's rapid passage, Askew wrote to former XIT division manager J. Ealy Moore of Dalhart and to Cordia Sloan Duke, the history-minded, diary-keeping widow of former XIT general manager Robert L. Duke, to propose organizing a reunion for XIT exes. When Moore and Mrs. Duke agreed with the idea, the three of them went on to organize the first gathering of old Panhandle cowboys.

Dalhart during the heyday of the giant XIT Ranch. *Author's collection.*

James D. Hamlin of Farwell, a lawyer who had represented the XIT in Texas since 1905, soon joined the reunion effort, along with Ace Hopper, who had worked as a cook on the XIT from 1892 to 1894.

"I just got tired of Gainesville and at twenty-two lit out for the Panhandle," Hopper later recalled. He soon became famous for once cooking forty-four breakfasts in as many minutes for hungry XIT cowboys. When he left the XIT, he settled in Plainview, and there he stayed

Meeting on October 20, 1936, in Fort Worth, the newly created XIT Reunion Association voted in Hamlin as "range boss." Askew would be secretary, Mrs. Duke would serve as historian and Hopper would be the reunion's official cook, overseeing a barbecue for all reunion attendees.

The next summer, the association staged its second reunion at Dalhart, then with five thousand residents and the nearest town to the old Buffalo Springs division headquarters. Pouring in by train and automobile, an onslaught of visitors tripled the size of the town. One reporter noted that it took a half hour to walk just one block.

The most-honored guest at the 1937 meeting was eighty-three-year-old Ab Blocker, who had come up from Bigwells in South Texas. As a trail driver for his brother, who had a ranch in Tom Green County, Blocker brought the first herd of cattle to the XIT in 1885. Not only did he deliver the ranch's first cattle, he also gave the ranch its famous brand.

Old XIT cowboys packed this hotel in Dalhart when they began an annual reunion in 1937. *XIT Ranch Museum, Dalhart, Texas.*

At the time, the ranch had no brand with which to mark its cattle. After figuring on the matter for a while, Blocker drew "XIT" in the dirt with his boot heel. That configuration could be burned with a straight iron and, if done carefully, could not be altered by rustlers. (That XIT stood for "Ten in Texas," since the ranch sprawled over parts of ten counties, has since been written off as legend.)

Also at the second meeting, the growing membership approved Dalhart as the permanent home of the reunion. But that vote was not unanimous. Representatives from Hereford and Littlefield argued for their towns, but Dalhart prevailed, largely due to a "rousing speech" by Mrs. Duke.

"Let's have the next meeting at Dalhart," she said, "the place nearest the first division of the XIT Ranch—Buffalo Springs. That's where the first calf was branded XIT, and a few cattle still bawl there, but thank God you won't hear any bawling wheat and cotton farmers."

Though no one was getting any younger, for a few years the number of old cowboys attending the reunion continued to grow as the event received more and more news media exposure, including national news reel coverage in 1939. Organizers estimated that roughly 1,500 cowboys and their wives qualified for membership, but ten times that many people of all ages and backgrounds showed up for the four-day event in the summer of 1941. The *Amarillo Globe-News* declared the annual gathering, by then in only its sixth year, the largest celebration in the United States based on the history of a ranch.

Every August, the old cowboys who came to Dalhart got to see a parade, eat barbecue, rattle their hocks at a dance and take in a rodeo regarded as one of the wildest anywhere. But the highlight of the annual get-together was the chance to get reacquainted with old friends and telling stories.

At the 1948 reunion, former trail boss J.G. "Potato" Owen explained to a young reporter how he came by his nickname. He had come to Texas from South Carolina at twenty-two, "a cowboy for to be," as the old expression had it. Working for the XIT, Owen thought his cowboys needed more grub than the cost-conscious owners furnished them.

Soon after a company bean counter showed up at the ranch from the head office in Chicago, Owen got summoned to ranch headquarters.

Once the cowboy took a seat in front of an officious, well-dressed auditor from the Windy City, the auditor asked Owen how many potatoes a cowboy could eat in a day.

"Don't know," Owen said after studying on it for a while, not wanting to waste words in front of a man who made his living counting things.

"Well," the moneyman said, "your cowboys have been eating twenty-one pounds a day. That's too many."

Turns out, Owen had been supplementing his cowboys' diet with canned goods and other food he charged simply as "potatoes."

As the years passed, the number of reunion attendees who had ridden for the brand began to wane, though the popularity of the event remained high. Of the original reunion organizers, Cordia Duke lived the longest. Late in her life, she collaborated with historian Dr. Joe B. Frantz on *Six Thousand Miles of Fence*, a book about the XIT published in 1961. Five years later, she died in Dalhart, where she had lived since her husband's death in 1933. The last old XIT waddy, Ira L. Taylor, died in an Amarillo nursing home in 1999 at the age of 102.

But the reunion, now more than three-quarters of a century in existence, has endured, still attracting thousands of visitors to Dalhart every summer.

CRITTERS

REMEMBERING BLACKIE

Nickels were not easily come by in the tough economic times of the early 1890s, but the cowboys who patronized Jim Scarborough's saloon in Claude never minded standing Blackie a drink when they could afford it.

When cowboys with a little time and money on their hands ventured into the saloon to order drinks, they'd usually find Blackie hanging out near the bar, looking on longingly. If no one offered him a beer, Blackie did not mind begging. Once he did that, making his big brown eyes look as pitiful as he could, it was generally more than a cowboy could take.

As soon as the bartender set down a cool bottle of brew on the bar, Blackie would stand, grab the bottle and down it to the last drop. He didn't say thanks, but his eyes and body language said it for him.

The reason Blackie didn't articulate his appreciation was that he was a bear. He liked his beer as much as any man, but bears couldn't talk.

If anything gave Blackie more pleasure than a bottle of beer, it was whipping up on the dogs belonging to the nesters who, thanks to the railroad, began pouring into the county. Often, one of those dogs would sniff out Blackie and pay a visit. Smart enough to know exactly how far his chain would reach, the bear would position himself so that he had plenty of loose chain to spare and wait with seeming indifference for one of the dogs to get within range. Then, to the delight of the cowboys who knew the drill, Blackie would box around the unsuspecting dog until it got loose and ran howling outside.

Years later, pioneer Panhandle rancher Jim Christian, who had spent fifteen years working on the famous JA Ranch in Armstrong County, told his daughter, Inez Christian Dozier of Amarillo, how Blackie came to be a fixture in early Claude.

"Several of us were gathering cattle north of Ceta Creek," he began. "Paul, my brother, was riding the hills and drifting the cattle toward the [Prairie Dog Town fork of the Red] river. I was working below and would gather the loose stuff and throw them into the main herd, which was farther down."

Christian heard his brother fire a shot about the same time he saw a large black bear running off through the brush. He figured his brother had only taken a potshot at the animal in the spirit of fun and continued tending to his business.

But when Christian got back to the herd, all the other cowboys were there except for Paul. When his brother finally rode into camp, he had a squiring baby bear in his hands. Annoyed with Jim for not coming to check on him after hearing the shot, Paul explained that he had run into a mother bear and two cubs. He decided to rope one of the babies. Naturally, the mama bear hadn't been too keen on the idea and put up a pretty good fight until Paul's shot ran her off with the other cub.

Paul took the cub to the ranch's Rush Creek Camp. The ranch manager and everyone else took a shine to the cub and collectively adopted him as the camp pet. The cowboys kept the bear chained to a cottonwood tree near the camp's rock well house.

"Blackie seemed contented enough, never wanting for food or entertainment," Christian continued. "The whole camp was beginning to feel very attached to him, and then, about the third morning, we found he had escaped."

Several days later, apparently coming to understand that he had a better deal at the ranch than he had first thought, the cub showed back up, content to be rechained as long as the groceries were forthcoming. Paul Christian formally conveyed the bear to be the pet of the young nephew of the ranch manager's wife, but after several months, the bear was regifted to the owner of the cowboys' favorite watering hole in Claude, Jim Scarborough.

Tame as he grew up to be, one trait he never overcame was his propensity to occasionally slip his chain and go for a walkabout in Claude. His favorite home away from home was the local hotel, where he became the nemesis of a middle-aged widow named Nellie Anderson Weaver.

"My, how that woman did dread that bear," Christian recalled, "for there was no compromising when he got a sniff of some favorite food."

One early morning, he said, Blackie absented himself from Scarborough's saloon and ambled over to the hotel. There he ran into Mrs. Weaver walking back from the barn with a fresh pail of milk.

"This was as gratifying a breakfast as he could imagine," Christian told his daughter. "But on raising his nose to the bucket, he found it held higher and higher. He was not to be denied, however, and he started climbing the indignant lady in his pursuit. Needless to say, he came out victorious."

While Blackie always had a robust appetite, he also enjoyed a refreshing dip in the rain barrel Mrs. Weaver kept just outside the hotel's dining room. Drinking water was not easy to come by back then, and Blackie's fondness for her rain barrel infuriated the lady hotelkeeper.

One day, busy rustling up lunch for her guests, Mrs. Weaver heard water splashing and immediately realized Blackie was cooling himself again in her rain barrel. Arming herself with a broom, she ran outside and began flailing away at Blackie every time he raised his head above the barrel rim.

"After churning out most of the water," former JA cowboy Charlie Taul later remembered, "[Blackie] darted out of the barrel and around the [hotel], sending a spray of water in the pathway of his pursuer. Noticing the front door ajar, he dodged in and on down the hall through the dining room, and then out the open window…into the rain barrel again."

Habits are hard to break, however, and Blackie continued to periodically get loose for a romp around town. One time that happened, a dog kept him on the run so long that he died from heat exhaustion.

"His pranks were the interest of the village and countryside," Christian concluded, "and even the hotel manager could not help pine at his going."

THE LAST BUFFALO

Endings are not always obvious at first.

Charlie Norris, a cowboy from Clayton, New Mexico, could have testified to that. It took about seven years before it finally sank in that he had seen the last substantial herd of buffalo in Texas.

To put the enormity of that into perspective, in the 1500s, when Spanish explorers first came to the Southwest, buffalo ranged over almost all of Texas. In 1850, the shaggy beasts still could be found in roughly half the state. Twenty years later, their range had decreased to the High Plains even though hundreds of thousands of them still thundered across the landscape. Only a decade after that, in 1880, the buffalo remaining in Texas could fit into a very small circle on the map in the Panhandle.

A buffalo hits the dust after taking a hunter's bullet. *Author's collection.*

In the spring of 1886, Norris rode up on that circle. Twenty years later, Ernest Thompson Seton preserved Norris's story in the October 1906 issue of *Scribner's Magazine.*

"I was driving a bunch of horses from Coldwater [in present Sherman County, long since a ghost town] to Buffalo Springs [in Dallam County], and when 35 miles east of Buffalo Springs," Norris told Seton, "saw the buffalo herd about three miles off. I knew at once they were buffalo, because they were all of one color."

Norris, who had been serving as guide, left the horses with their owner at their destination and went about his business. The next day, heading back west, he saw the herd about fifteen miles from the point he had first seen it.

"I rode in among them, some were lying down and some were grazing," he recalled, estimating the herd amounted to about two hundred head.

When the animals saw Norris, he continued, they bunched like cattle and started milling around. Norris watched as a succession of bulls tried to interest the herd in stampeding, but the herd seemed to have little spirit for it.

"I galloped behind trying to rope a calf, but the mother turned on me," Norris said. "I had no gun, my horse was tired, so I gave up."

Norris rode on to his outfit's camp, about fifteen miles from the buffalo. The camp had been set up near a small lake, the only water in the area.

Two days later, the herd showed up at the water hole. "They drank very heavily, and then played about like calves," Norris said.

After watching them for a while, Norris killed a cow, and his range boss killed a bull. Then they roped three calves. When the mother of the third calf tried to defend her offspring, someone shot and killed her.

One of the calves died fairly soon after its capture, another ended up in Charles Goodnight's herd in Palo Duro Canyon and the third got traded to someone riding through from Kansas for "a span of colts."

That November, Norris had occasion to pass through the area again. This time he saw only twelve head and never saw another buffalo in the Panhandle after that.

Norris later learned that someone killed four buffalo at Buffalo Springs in 1889, "the very last individuals that I have knowledge of."

Seton closed his article with a big question and an answer reflective of the times. "Why was it allowed?" he wrote, referring to the virtual extinction of the species. "Why did the government not act?"

Then Seton offered this: "There is one answer—the extermination was absolutely inevitable…It had to be; he [the buffalo] served his time and now his time is past."

That's a hard answer, but the only alternative would have been keeping about one-fourth of the continent as one vast game preserve.

Antelope Still Home on the Range in the Panhandle

No thanks to Lester B. Colby and anyone else who may have done what he did, thousands of pronghorn antelope are still home on the range in the Panhandle.

Colby, who in 1912 wrote an article on the Panhandle for a long-defunct monthly called the *Texas Magazine*, probably was an OK fellow. Even so, he did something—and openly wrote about it in his five-page story—that likely would land him in jail today, not to mention netting him a big fine.

His offense involved using unfair and arguably cruel means to hunt pronghorns. If he reflected at all on his actions, he must have believed that the species would always exist in vast numbers. That, or he simply didn't care.

The cocky young magazine writer certainly did not stand alone as the only early-day Texan to take the state's wildlife, particularly antelope, for granted.

Years before Colby wrote his Panhandle piece, an army officer lately returned to Washington, D.C., from duty in Texas wrote to a "Professor C. Stemms" in Austin saying that his friends at the Smithsonian Institution had been disappointed that he had not brought them "some specimens of the natural history of Texas, something of the bug, reptile, fish, etc. species."

If the good professor would send some critters to assist "their efforts in the advancement of science," the military man continued, Smithsonian scientists "will send you copies of all the scientific papers published by their institution and give you credit in their papers for all information and specimens."

The Smithsonian had a particular interest in obtaining a stuffed antelope for its collection since there was "not one to be seen in any of the museums in the United States."

Referring to a couple of their Texas acquaintances, the officer continued, "Can you not get Polly or King to kill one and have it sent to me?"

Whether Stemms followed through is not known, but Texas had no shortage of antelope in those days, even if the nation's museums did. Numbering in the scores of thousands, antelope roamed two-thirds of Texas, as common as deer.

A bit of humor published in one newspaper in the late 1880s reflects the long-standing attitude of many toward the species, which only the buffalo, for a time, had outnumbered on the High Plains: "'I should be pleased to meat you,' said the hungry hunter to the antelope, which stood just out of reach. 'No, thank you,' said the antelope. 'I've too much at steak.'"

By 1907, when Colby took a five-hundred-mile automobile tour of the Panhandle before it had any paved roads, Texas's antelope herd had been reduced by overhunting and pushed farther west. Still, the fast-running, tan-and-white ungulates could be found in the Panhandle and Trans-Pecos.

Near Tahoka, using his car as a horse, Colby and a local cowboy went antelope hunting.

"It is hard to imagine a sport more exciting than running down an antelope with an automobile," he wrote.

Part of the thrill came from the terrain. Even though flat and open, as Colby put it, there were "some bumps" on the high plains. "Badgers and prairie dogs dig holes," he wrote, "and now and then there [are] the remains of an old buffalo wallow."

Meanwhile, back to the chase...

"For the first two or three miles the animal will distance the average car," Colby reported. (Indeed, antelope run as fast as seventy miles an hour.) "At

Pronghorn antelope nearly followed the buffalo to extinction in the Panhandle. *Author's collection.*

the end of 10 miles the antelope, no matter how good a runner…is no longer a bobbing spot against the horizon. Gradually, the machine overcomes the fleeing flesh."

After a pursuit that Colby estimated at thirty miles, the antelope began to lag. Finally, he wrote, "a cowboy in the car lassoed him as neatly as he could have caught a steer from a pony's back."

Colby did not explain in his story what happened next, but the long-ago magazine article includes two photographs of him posing next to his spoke-wheeled runabout holding a dead buck by its horns and white tail.

A decade later, the *Hansford Headlight* informed readers in its part of the Panhandle that a new state law intended to protect pronghorns from extinction had gone on the books. Effective June 10, 1917, the hunting of antelope was prohibited in Texas for the next quarter century, but the prohibition on hunting already dated to 1903. That meant Colby's hunt in 1907 was illegal, though the state had only a few game wardens back then.

The measure worked. On a permit basis depending on herd size, pronghorn hunting resumed in 1944 and has continued since then. But you still can't chase and lasso them from a car.

Law and Disorder

Dead Duck Triggers a Gun Battle

It all started over a duck.

Caleb Berg (Cape) Willingham, first sheriff of newly organized Oldham County, happened to be in the Equity Bar, Tascosa's oldest saloon, when he heard a commotion outside. Suddenly, one of the town's few ladies did something most ladies of the era would not: she ran into the drinking establishment.

"He killed my duck!" the woman yelled, pointing to a man outside. "Shot it just now."

Willingham saw that the woman was referring to Fred Leigh, foreman on the LS Ranch. Leigh was known for his drinking and had been warned before about carrying a pistol in town.

"He did, did he?" the sheriff asked. "Well, now, don't you worry. I'll see that the gentleman pays you for your duck."

Armed with a double-barreled shotgun, the big sheriff walked out and approached the cowboy to discuss the fair market value of domesticated migratory waterfowl.

"You're in debt to this woman for that duck you shot just now," the sheriff said. "You going to pay for it?"

"Hell, no, I ain't going to pay for no duck," the cowboy replied.

Willingham was in the process of reminding the cowboy that he was sheriff when he saw the drover's hand moving toward the six-shooter on his hip. That ended the talking. The sheriff let loose with both barrels of his scattergun. With eighteen pieces of buckshot in his body, the cowboy tumbled from his horse, as dead as the duck he'd blasted a short time before.

This illustration from an old western magazine depicts wild and wooly Tascosa in the 1880s. *Author's collection.*

Not only had Leigh been killed on account of a duck, but he also had the added distinction of being the first person buried on a hill outside Tascosa that soon bore one of the most famous names in the Old West. Leigh having died with his boots on, saloon proprietor Jack Ryan thought it fitting that the new graveyard be called Boothill. (Dodge City also had a Boothill, but that was way off in Kansas.)

Willingham went on to serve out his term as sheriff, but in 1882 he was defeated in his bid for another two years in office. After losing the election, Willingham moved east across the Panhandle to Wheeler County, where he operated a saloon in Mobeetie. Later, he became manager of the Turkey Track Ranch.

Without mentioning his sources, J. Marvin Hunter described Leigh's death in an article he wrote for his *Frontier Times* magazine in 1943. Three years later, Amarillo writer John McCarthy told the story a little differently in his book *Maverick Town: The Story of Old Tascosa*.

In McCarthy's version, the woman who owned the duck was pregnant. She fainted after seeing Leigh shoot off the bird's head. McCarthy also listed

Leigh as the second occupant of Boothill, not the first. But both authors agreed that it all started over a duck.

Hunter said the shooting happened in 1879, but Willingham had not become sheriff until 1880. McCarthy did not offer a date in his book.

No matter when exactly Leigh died, or whether he was permanent guest number one or number two, Boothill Cemetery went on to accommodate a total of thirty-two graves. Twenty-three of the occupants were men who, like Leigh, died with their boots on.

The names of some of Boothill's residents have long since been forgotten, men like the character later remembered only as "the Colonel." No one knew too much about him other than that he dressed well and made his living playing cards. Like many men in the days of the Old West, he didn't talk much about his past, though folks in Tascosa figured he had seen hard service on one side or the other during the Civil War. That's how come he came to be called the colonel. The other thing they

The original Oldham County Courthouse in Tascosa, now a museum on Cal Farley's Boy's Ranch. *Photo by Bill G. Cox.*

A youngster in the 1960s enjoys a popsicle alongside the historical marker at Tascosa, scene of many a wild shootout. *Photo by Bill G. Cox.*

noticed is that when gunplay erupted in town—which it often did, if only a cowboy firing off a few rounds in the air—the colonel seemed unusually affected by the noise.

The colonel made a good, if not honest, living on his dexterous dealing. But one night, a Frying Pan Ranch cowboy whose blood alcohol level should have rendered him much less observant saw the colonel deal one from the bottom of the deck. How useful a card it happened to be or what suit it represented went unrecorded, but seeing no need to delay the game by calling a misdeal, the ranch hand whipped out his pistol and put a hole just below the colonel's heart. The colonel saw the weapon before it went off, but even though he had a reputation for being fast on the draw, he made no effort to clear leather with his own piece.

Maybe the colonel, having endured the horrors of war, suffered from the psychological condition that would come to be known as posttraumatic stress disorder. Maybe he felt badly about all the card players he'd cheated since turning to that profession. Or maybe he suffered from depression and

The historical marker at the old Tascosa's Boothill Cemetery.
Photo by Mike Cox.

self-medicated with too much booze. For whatever reason, as he fell forward in his chair, onlookers heard him say only two words: "Thank God!"

Tascosa, like most of the people in its cemetery, did not live to enjoy old age. When the Fort Worth and Denver Railroad cut across the Panhandle, the tracks did not come to Tascosa. The once lively—and deadly—cow town faded away as the nearby railroad town of Amarillo grew.

In 1893, a flood on the Canadian River destroyed the bridge leading into town, as well as many buildings. That was the last straw for Tascosa, which eventually lost its county seat status to Vega. The same year, Willingham left the Panhandle for New Mexico. He ran a ranch near Roswell before continuing west to Arizona. He died there in 1925 at the age of seventy-two.

Today, all that remains of old Tascosa—now the home of Cal Farley's Boy's Ranch—is the rock building that once served as the courthouse and a hilltop collection of lonely graves.

R.G. MILLER'S BIG DAY WAS HIS LAST

Fifty-six years later, Ben Andis still clearly remembered the events of that early summer day.

One thing that stood out in his mind was the temperature. For that time of the year in the Texas Panhandle, it was warmer than normal—downright hot.

Trains had been bringing people into Clarendon all morning. Wagons, buggies and people on horseback and afoot jammed the streets. With all the excitement, it seemed like the Fourth of July, but it was a month earlier—June 3, 1910. A holiday atmosphere certainly prevailed, but the occasion was different.

Out in the nearby sand hills, fourteen-year-old Andis had been working since early morning on a crew operating a horse-drawn grader on a county road. The commotion in town finally got to the point that the foreman told his crew to take off.

The horse that had been pulling the grader was hitched to a buggy, and Andis and several others went to join the crowd. When they got as close as they could, Andis stood on the floorboard of the buggy to get a better view.

As he watched, the crowd parted to allow six men through. The procession included a Catholic priest, a Protestant minister, the sheriff and two of his deputies and the guest of honor, a tall man in a dark suit. His name was G.R. Miller, and this was his big day—his last.

For reasons not clearly understood, Miller had killed two railroad hoboes and wounded two others. The killings happened as he fled Clarendon on a freight train after stealing a pistol from a friend and blowing up another acquaintance's house with dynamite. Clearly, Miller was not a happy citizen of Donley County.

All that happened in March 1909. That November, Miller got a life sentence for one of the murders and the death penalty for the second. District judge J.N. Browning sentenced him to hang on June 3, "not earlier than 11:00 a.m. and no later than sundown."

As was customary, the sheriff allowed the condemned man a few parting remarks. Miller gave a little talk from the gallows, observing that while it was too late to be "crying over split milk," he hoped that all the children in the crowd "will be good children."

After he concluded his talk, the sheriff put a black hood over Miller's head, adjusted the noose around his neck and stepped back. The trapdoor sprung, and Miller's sentence was carried out. The drop space was shielded by wooden planks.

Though Andis was already doing a man's work, by modern standards—and law—he still was a boy. Seeing the hanging clearly made an impression on the youngster. True to Miller's injunction about being good, Andis went into law enforcement.

In 1966, more than a half century after the hanging, Andis continued to do good for people as chief deputy sheriff for Potter County sheriff Paul Gaither. The hanging he witnessed as a teenager had been the last legal execution by that means in the Panhandle. Times had changed, but not man's ability to choose between good and evil.

CLARENDON'S "COWARDLY" CONSTABLE

O.H. Finch first saw the Texas Panhandle in 1892 from the caboose of a freight train hauling two cars of bulls from Burlingame, Kansas, to his father's ranch in Donley County, the Bar Ninety Six.

Reaching Panhandle City on the Santa Fe, the twelve-year-old Finch and his father took the Fort Worth and Denver train to Washburn. From there, they rode to Salisbury, the nearest post office to their vast ranch.

More than a half century later, Finch wrote about his experiences in a now-scarce, self-published family history, *The Lives and Times of a Family Named Finch*. In his book, he told of an incident that convinced him Texas remained the Wild West.

When their train stopped for breakfast at Clarendon, Finch and his father walked from the depot to a restaurant across the street. As they ate, Finch recalled, "My eyes popped open wide when a man stepped out of this place with two guns, one hanging on either side. It was Jim Green, sheriff of the county." (Elected on November 4, 1890, Green actually served as Precinct 2 constable.)

Finch had never seen, as he put it, "a wild and woolly Texan." Then thirty-six, Green had dark hair, brown eyes and a dark complexion. He stood six feet tall. His hat, boots and the fact that he had once ridden as a Texas Ranger made him seem ever taller to the boy from Kansas.

But Green's career as a state lawman had gotten off to a shaky start.

"When he with other Rangers got into his first encounter with law breakers, and the shooting started, he could not stand the gaff, and he broke and ran," Finch wrote, crediting the story to Will Beverly, the 1890s foreman of the Rowe Ranch in Donley County. "His fellow Rangers chided him but they knew he wasn't a coward."

The Lives and Times of a Family Named Finch, a rare, privately published book on a pioneer Panhandle ranching family, first told the story of the cowardly ranger who died bravely. *Photo by Mike Cox.*

Indeed, Green asked for another chance to "show that he could take it." When that next opportunity came, the young ranger "shut both his eyes and began to shoot."

To what extent shooting blind affected his marksmanship went unsaid, but the ranger survived the encounter and "proved his mettle many times afterwards."

Green served in the Texas Rangers for eighteen months, leaving effective August 31, 1882. He had worked under Company B, Captain George Washington Arrington, and later for Company C, Captain Sam McMurry. After leaving the rangers, he stayed in law enforcement, though it's unclear where he wore a badge prior to his election in Clarendon.

Finch didn't recall the date in his book, but on July 5, 1892, the former ranger got one last chance to prove that he had long since stiffened his backbone when it came to doing his job as a peace officer.

That came when the Bell boys—Bob, Gene and Wally—arrived in Clarendon on the morning train. The three brothers were, as Finch characterized them, "notorious gamblers in Amarillo." And they had a standing grudge against the former ranger.

In a scene later repeated in many Westerns, the three hard cases removed themselves to one of the town's saloons and began boozing it up. The boys made no attempt to conceal their identity. In fact, they let it be known, as country western singer Marty Robbins sang decades later in his classic ballad "Big Iron," that there was an ex-ranger who "wouldn't be too long in town."

When Green walked into the saloon that morning, Finch wrote, "the shooting began."

The ex-ranger, no longer needing to work his pistol with his eyes closed, put a bullet into one of the Bells before another of the brothers shot him. From the wooden floor, the dying Green shot again and killed a second brother. Now only Wally stood, and he found it expedient to vacate the saloon.

"This caused a lot of excitement since three men were killed before breakfast," Finch understated.

A Donley County history published in 1975 devotes only two paragraphs to the shooting but tells the story a little differently:

> Green and the Bells had some trouble over Green's shooting Bill Bell in May of that year and the brothers called his hand. All three drew and fired. Robert Bell fell dead but Eugene shot Green. Another unforeseen fatality occurred when a stranger who had just arrived on the early morning train entered the swinging doors of the saloon just in time to catch a stray bullet and was killed instantly.

That man was George Bingham Grissom, a Texas and Southwestern Cattlemen's Association inspector. Born in Tennessee in 1858, Grissom came with his family to Denton County as a youngster. Following his death in Clarendon, his body was shipped to Denton County for burial in the Bolivar Cemetery at Sanger.

The final resting place of the ex-ranger who overcame his fear of gunplay only to die with his boots on has not been located. Neither has the grave of the man he killed.

CLAIREMONT AND ITS OLD JAIL

A noted outlaw, the story goes, lies on his deathbed mortally wounded by a Texas Ranger's well-placed .45 slug.

"Tell me who you rode with and where I can find 'em," the state lawman orders the dying bad man.

"Can you keep a secret?" the pale felon whispers, barely able to talk.

"You bet your boots I can," the ranger replies.

"So can I," the outlaw says shortly before dying with his boots on.

And so can the graffiti-covered old jail in what little is left of the South Plains community of Clairemont, once the seat of Kent County.

Named after Alamo defender Andrew Kent, the county was organized in 1892. A land dealer named R.L. Rhomberg donated a town site for a county seat named in honor of a young family member, Claire Becker.

A two-story courthouse with an attic and cupola became the hub of a new community that soon featured all the amenities, from general store to post office to livery stable.

In 1895, county officials had the jail built of red sandstone quarried from a feature called Treasure Butte southeast of town on the 0-0 Ranch. The

Its old jail is about all that's left of Clairemont. *Photo by Mike Cox.*

first floor of the eighteen- by twenty-four-foot building held a steel cage containing four cells. While a state-of-the-art facility in every other regard, the new lockup did not feature indoor plumbing and never did. Inmates had to use an outhouse.

For their money, Kent County taxpayers got themselves a sturdy slammer, known across West Texas as virtually escape-proof. In fact, local lore has it that only one inmate ever made it outside of his own volition—except to go to the outhouse.

The prisoner somehow managed to get out of the jail and hotfoot it across the street, where he ran up the stairs in the courthouse and hid in the cupola atop the building. After going without food for a couple days while the sheriff and others searched for him, the hungry escapee decided a meal behind bars beat freedom and a growling stomach.

What got him in the clink in the first place is not mentioned in the telling of the story in Jewell Pritchett and Erma Black's 1983 book, *Kent County and Its People.*

Kent County must have had its share of miscreants and felons over the years, not to mention unwelcome visitors up to no good, but the nature of crime in the county goes unreported in their book. While acknowledging that their county once had "a wild and tough reputation" and had seen many "brutal crimes" in its early history, the authors wrote, "These stories have been told repeatedly by fledgling writers who often glorified the evil deeds done to make the sensational stories even more gruesome and gory than was factual."

Those crimes, the authors continued, included "cowardly murders, where the victim was shot in the back" and the occasional lynching. And it does not strain credulity to suppose that at one time or another someone might even have rustled a cow or two or "borrowed" a horse and forgot to return it.

"Those dark days are gone," the county historian concluded, "and old enmities are best forgotten. We do not care to stir up any new problems nor to open closet doors long since sealed."

That sentiment may explain why the old jail has no official state historical marker to tell visitors anything about its history. Across the highway, in front of what's left of the old courthouse, is a granite marker commemorating Kent County's ninetieth anniversary. But the polished stone offers no details other than a listing of the original county officials and does not mention the old jail or why both buildings stand abandoned and vulnerable to vandals.

In fact, the biggest crime in Clairemont history may have been the "theft" of its status as county seat, an event that transformed it into the ghost town it is today.

When a rail line came through the county in 1909, it bypassed Clairemont by ten miles in favor of the community of Jayton. Clairemont slowly declined while Jayton grew. In 1952, county residents voted to move the county seat to Jayton. The courthouse and jail stood abandoned by 1954.

Not long after county officials moved their offices to Jayton, a fire heavily damaged the old courthouse. The county had what was left of the second story removed and restored the first floor for use as a community center. The Clairemont post office finally closed in 1970 with the retirement of the last postmaster.

As for Kent County's "dark days," until someone takes the time to wade through rolls of newspaper microfilm and pore over the county's criminal dockets, assuming those records have remained intact, the old jail's secrets will keep.

"KID" MURRAY

Newspapers dubbed Texas's least-known outlaw "Kid" Murray.

By 1903, the Old West lived mostly in the imaginations of people who read dime novels or went to the newfangled moving picture shows. Still, the sense of frontier endured in some areas, particularly the Panhandle.

Though only the bones of buffalo littered the plains and the blue-clad cavalry had ridden out of Fort Elliott in Wheeler County in 1890, that part of Texas remained lightly settled in the first decade of the twentieth century. Crisscrossed with barbed wire, this vast grassland had far more cattle than people.

An outlaw named Murray found those conditions to his liking. With impunity, he stole horses and cattle from Panhandle ranchers. As angry owners and frustrated lawmen began combing the country for the talented rustler, he went on the lam.

Eventually, a Wheeler County sheriff's deputy tracked him down, possibly in Indian Territory (now Oklahoma). During the pursuit, Murray shot and wounded an officer, though a spare newspaper account printed downstate in Austin offers no details.

Unlike that other "Kid," one William (Billy) Bonney, little is known about Kid Murray. But one thing stands out even more than a century after the exploits that got his name in the newspapers: he was only eleven years old.

So who was "Kid" Murray? Obviously, he was a boy who grew up in a hurry—a child "man" enough to ride a horse, herd cattle and handle a

Teenage outlaw "Kid" Murray spent time in the Wheeler County Jail, built in 1886 when the Panhandle remained sparsely settled. *Photo by Mike Cox.*

gun. He could have been an orphan or an errant runaway. Maybe even a loving couple's son. The imagination presents numerous possibilities. But the next several issues of the newspaper offer no follow-up story, leaving the questions unanswered.

At only eleven, the "Kid" probably got a second chance. Many a captured horse thief ended up dangling from a tree limb, but Texans were softer on their young. Most parents did not spare the proverbial rod when it came to disciplining their offspring, but few could abide the notion of putting a kid behind bars with older hard cases.

As early as the 1850s, state lawmakers had realized that children should not be treated the same as adult offenders. The legislature passed a statute exempting anyone under thirteen from criminal prosecution and approved a separate institution to house wayward children adjudicated for delinquent conduct. But the sectional friction that turned into the Civil War soon put matters of juvenile justice on the governmental back burner.

Some three decades went by before any further progress occurred in Texas. Finally understanding that it did little good to send a youthful felon to the state prison in Huntsville, in 1887 the legislature passed a law creating the first juvenile rehabilitation facility in the South. The House of Correction and Reformatory (later better known as the Gatesville School for Boys) opened in Coryell County in January 1889.

After an initial stay in the Wheeler County Jail in Mobeetie, the "Kid" likely ended up in Gatesville, though records from that era are sketchy, and no paperwork proving the disposition of his case has been located. It is known that as of August 31, 1904, Texas had 3,975 felons in custody, more than 700 of them younger than twenty, and some under fifteen.

Did the system succeed in straightening up Kid Murray, or did he continue down a road that eventually led him to Huntsville or on a last walk to the gallows? With such a common surname, his trail has proven hard to find.

He would have been born in 1891 or 1892, meaning he easily could have lived well into the twentieth century, possibly into the 1970s or '80s. If he settled down, it was not in Wheeler County. Online cemetery records contain no deceased person named Murray whose age would have matched his.

Whoever he was, the "Kid" made history. As the short newspaper piece touching on his crime and apprehension concluded, "He is believed to be the most youthful criminal who has ever figured in the criminal history."

MYSTERIES

PALO DURO MYSTERY MAN

The story of the Palo Duro Canyon wild man spread across Texas by rail.

Maybe the *Dallas Morning News* reporter had been hanging around the depot, taking note of all the detraining passengers in the journalistic style of the day, or maybe he had been routinely checking the registers at the city's various hotels, looking for names that ought to be in the news. However it happened, the enterprising journalist ran into W.C. Keegle, lately arrived from the Texas Panhandle, and turned the encounter into a story his newspaper published on February 15, 1886.

The reporter didn't offer any background on Keegle, noting only that he and another man had been the ones who first encountered a mysterious man living alone in the vastness of Palo Duro Canyon, a tortured soul who seemed to have a figurative skeleton in his closet. The tale, the journalist predicted, would "live to cheer the fancy of future Palodurans." Actually, the story appears to have been completely forgotten since its initial publication.

When the reporter asked Keegle if he'd tell him what he knew about the Palo Duro wild man, Keegle replied, "Oh, I do not care to refer to him. The people would say that I was dreaming, and I do not care for that class of notoriety."

A bystander, to whom the reporter referred only as "a third party," urged Keegle to go ahead and tell all. "Perhaps it will have the effect of scaring off the grass commissioners," he said, a reference to the then-current controversy over grazing rights on the still vast amount of public lands in the Panhandle.

At that, Keegle let loose with his story.

The furtive Palo Duro mystery man was seen near this waterfall in the canyon. *Author's collection.*

It traced back to April 1878, not quite three years after Colonel Ranald MacKenzie forced the Panhandle's last hostile band of Comanche out of their perennial stronghold in Palo Duro during the Red River War of 1874–75.

"I was encamped in the canyon cutting out timber for Gunter & Munson, of Sherman, with which to fence their range," Keegle said. "Except myself and my assistant, there was not as we thought a human voice to wake the echoes of that part of the canyon."

Indeed, except for the area around a roaring twenty-five-foot waterfall on the Prairie Dog Town Fork of the Red River, the silence in the long, wide canyon was "unfathomable."

Despite all the quietude, as the days went on and their stack of cedar posts grew higher, the two men realized their supply of food seemed to be decreasing at a rate that exceeded even their hardy appetites. In short, someone or some critter somehow was surreptitiously sharing their grub. The two men increased their vigilance, but during the day while they were out working, the raider would invariably hit their larder.

"The theft was kept up for about nine weeks," Keegle recalled, "during which the identity of the thief was involved in mystery, for there was no reason to believe that any living human being lurked in the haunted precincts of the canyon." (Judging from this quote, the reporter apparently felt obliged to help the reluctant Keegle spice up his tale a bit.)

Since the two Gunter & Munson employees knew they were the only humans in that part of the canyon, they suspected the thief might have four legs. Perhaps the offender was a raccoon, a naturally bandit-faced animal known for its intelligence. But if so, the animal left no tracks or mess.

The mystery continued until, one day, Keegle's helper jumped a strange man who ran when he tried to approach. The two men made an effort to trail the fellow, who was clad only in tattered skins tied together, but they couldn't find him.

Even so, following that encounter, the steady disappearance of their groceries stopped.

There was more to the story, but Keegle said he preferred that his friend, indentified only as "Mr. Browne," tell the rest of it.

"The supposition is that the man was a penitent," Browne began. However, he continued, some of the few facts they had made a case for lunacy.

After that first, if short-lived, confrontation, the two men spotted the mystery man several other times.

Prairie Dog Town fork of the
Red River in Palo Duro Canyon.
Author's collection.

Devil's Tombstone in
Palo Duro Canyon.
Author's collection.

"As soon as he discovered that he was observed," Browne went on, "he would fly with almost superhuman speed." One time they did find a set of tracks and followed them several miles along the river before losing them.

In telling others on Charles Goodnight's JA Ranch about what they had seen, they found that one of Goodnight's cowboys had also encountered the man. The ranch hand got close enough to overhear the man muttering prayers of forgiveness "in the language of wild despair, and saying that his soul was gangrened and mortified, and then he would curse the railroads."

Then the tone of the man's entreaties changed as he began raving about being chased by a man on a mule. As the cowboy watched, the man began brandishing a thick piece of wood as if to ward off something only he could see.

"This was the only time…the poor man was overheard communing with his great secret, whatever that was," Browne continued. "About then… and for some time afterward the roars of an affrighted man seemingly running for his life—a sound between a scream and a dismal wailing—were occasionally heard in the canyon."

That cry of terror, heard "under the white moon, in the calm distinctness of the rocks and trees, was terrible beyond description," Browne said.

Goodnight's cowboy, an old hand at tracking strays, easily followed the man's trail. Suddenly, he saw a new set of tracks, those of a shod mule. The cowboy reported what he had seen to Goodnight, who returned to investigate. He, too, found mule tracks in a part of the canyon where no mules were known to be, especially shod mules.

And there the story ended. After that, the mystery man was never seen again.

Lubbock's Memphis Man and Other Spooks

Mac Davis and his "happiness is Lubbock in my rearview mirror" line to the contrary, the Hub City of the Plains has a lot going for it. There's exciting college football in the fall, the Buddy Holly museum, the world's largest collection of vintage windmills and plenty of friendly residents.

As windy as it can be, especially in the spring, Lubbock doesn't seem like a place that would have any particular appeal to ethereal apparitions, but Rob Weiner, a librarian at Texas Tech University, begs to differ. Speaking at the 2011 meeting of the West Texas Historical Association, he offered two Lubbock ghost stories and one strange tale of a man who made his amends for a ghastly crime one brick at a time.

Before getting started, Weiner stressed that, so far as he knew, none of the local legends has any basis in fact. He moved to Lubbock with his family when he was ten, first heard the stories as a kid and has continued to hear them as an adult, he said. None of them has ever been published.

The first tale centers on a nameless Lubbock doctor of long ago who, despite his Hippocratic oath, didn't care much for kids. In fact, the story goes, this particular MD disliked children so much that he took to killing them.

The not-so-kindly physician didn't go around town overtly doing away with children, of course. But when kids ended up in his hospital, a worrisome

Lubbock's Memphis Man supposedly hangs out at the intersection where he was killed: Sixty-sixth and Memphis. *Photo by Mike Cox.*

percentage of them never made it home. They mysteriously died during treatment. Even tonsillectomies tended to have tragic outcomes.

In a twist that only makes sense in folk tales, the good bad doctor covered his evil tracks by burying his clinical "mistakes" on the hospital grounds.

The killer physician's malevolent malpractice continued until the ghosts of his young victims, demonstrating surprising awareness of the ancient "eye-for-an-eye, tooth-for-a-tooth" philosophical concept, in some way killed the doctor. And even though their work on earth was done, the baby ghosts continued to hang around the hospital watching over other kids admitted to the facility. Just in case.

"This story is never associated with any particular hospital," Weiner said. "But I've heard it for years."

Weiner's next tale centers on a suburban Lubbock residence locally known as the "Prison Man's House."

Since someone still lives there, the address will go unreported. But anyone happening to drive by is likely to notice something strikingly unusual about the one-story brick house: it does not at all match the other houses in the neighborhood. What it looks very much like is a prison unit, minus the bars.

The legend is that back in the 1940s, a man killed his wife. While duly arrested and convicted of murder, the man drew prison time in lieu of the death penalty. But he got released from Huntsville on some manner of legal loophole and returned to the free world.

Having grown remorseful during his time behind bars, the man came to the conclusion that on the cosmic scheme of things, he still had a debt to pay for doing away with his significant other. So, legend has it, he built his own personal prison.

"The way the house looks lends to the mythology," Weiner said. "Whoever built it just kept building on, the result being a pretty dreadful-looking place very reminiscent of a prison."

Photos Weiner took of the house through his car window show a low-slung, rambling, reddish-orange brick structure with high, narrow, rectangular windows. All in all, the house presents a decidedly institutional look.

Though the Prison Man's House is still occupied, its builder has long since gone to face a higher tribunal in the death of his wife, leaving behind only his grim architecture and an unusual legend.

Finally, Weiner told the tale of the "Memphis Man."

First, some geographical background: Lubbock is an easy city to get around in. Most of the east–west streets are numbered, 1st through 146th. Most of the north–south avenues are designated with letters or proper nouns (mainly states and cities) in alphabetical order, starting with Avenue A on the east side of town and moving toward Quaker Avenue on the west.

Memphis Street, then, is a north–south thoroughfare that intersects various numbered streets, including Sixty-sixth. It is at this intersection where a ghost known as the Memphis Man supposedly hangs out.

According to Weiner, a Lubbock man who preferred leaving the driving to others patiently stood at that corner waiting on a city bus one icy winter morning only to end up catching a free ride to a destination he had not had in mind. As the bus approached, the large vehicle skidded on the ice and crashed into the hapless commuter, who in trying to save gas, lost his life.

The traffic fatality, with the assistance of an optical illusion, eventually gave rise to the local legend that the intersection was not only busy but also haunted.

"If you're driving north on Memphis, when you get to that intersection, it looks like there's a man leaning on a utility post near the bus stop," Weiner said. "But when you get closer, you see it's just a circuit breaker near the pole."

That completely logical explanation aside, it's a lot more fun to envision some poor spirit forever waiting on a bus at Memphis and Sixty-sixth.

The Wind

Wind Wagons

Perhaps H.M. Fletcher grew as tired of buying feed for the horses that pulled his wagon as future generations of Texans would weary of high gasoline prices. Could be he figured he might make some money. Or maybe he just decided to have a little fun.

Whatever his inspiration, the Plainview man took action on an idea he believed would put Old Dobbin to pasture for good: a wagon that did not require four-legged energy. He was not alone in thinking about other ways to get around, of course. Already, horseless carriages powered by gasoline engines competed with buggies and wagons on the nation's streets and unpaved roadways.

But Fletcher envisioned a different sort of horseless carriage, one that did not rely on fossil fuel. His invention would harness as its power source one of nature's elemental forces: the wind.

Sometime in 1910, Fletcher pulled a wagon into his barn, laid out his tools and went to work. What emerged definitely got the attention of his Hale County neighbors. In fact, folks were still talking about it seventy years later.

Using the wind as a means of locomotion was not a new idea. Man had been plying the seas and rivers in sailing vessels for centuries. Even using the wind to propel a wagon was not an original concept.

In 1853, entrepreneur William Thomas demonstrated a wind-powered prairie schooner to the U.S. Army at Fort Leavenworth in what was then the Kansas Territory. Thomas's invention extended twenty-five feet in length. It had twelve-foot wheels and a single sail on a seven-foot mast.

Cartoon by Roger Moore.

Thomas envisioned a fleet of sailing wagons rolling along the Santa Fe Trail, moving people and goods across the plains. But as one historian later put it, when the prototype wind wagon crashed, Thomas's potential financial backers became Doubting Thomases and pulled their support. The would-be CEO of the Overland Navigation Co. blew out of Kansas sans windfall.

Samuel Peppard of Jefferson County, Kansas, became the next creative thinker to build a wind wagon. The upshot of his 1860 effort is best summarized by what folks soon called it: Peppard's Folly.

A half century later in the Texas Panhandle, Fletcher concluded that hoisting a sail on a wagon was the wrong approach. If windmills could suck water out of the earth, he reasoned, they could power a wagon.

So, Fletcher raised a windmill in the back of a wagon. If he made any drawings of his invention, they are not known today. This much is surmised: gears connected to the sucker rod somehow turned the wheels. He also developed a steering system.

As late as the 1970s, a few old-timers in the Panhandle remembered having heard about the wind wagon. They said Fletcher's big moment came when he climbed on his windmill wagon and tried to ride his invention from Plainview to Amarillo.

He made it as far as Canyon, about thirty miles south of Amarillo. North of town, a hill proved insurmountable.

L.L. Roser, eight years old in 1910, told a correspondent for the *Amarillo Globe-News* in 1981 that he had seen the wind wagon.

"It was just a regular windmill on an ordinary wagon," Roser said. "The wagon didn't have any specially built bed, and the windmill wasn't the biggest there was, although it did make the wagon move."

Another old-timer, Harold Hamilton, told the Amarillo newspaper that he also remembered seeing Fletcher's contraption.

"Mr. Fletcher also was going to plow with it if it developed properly," he said.

Fletcher's invention did not require grain or gas to roll across the High Plains, but it did need wind. A strong breeze is common enough in the Panhandle, but still days do occur. And on those days, the owner of a wind wagon would be as becalmed as any clipper ship with sagging sail.

Not only did Fletcher's idea never catch on, his out-of-the-box-but-in-the-wagon-bed thinking never got the attention accorded his predecessors in the wind wagon field. The misadventures of Thomas and Peppard, the original High Plains drifters, fueled folklore (Walt Disney did a short animated feature called *Windwagon Smith* in 1961), fiction and nonfiction, but Fletcher and his windmill wagon have been forgotten.

RACING THE WIND

In 1900, it had not occurred to anyone in the Panhandle that pursuing a tornado would someday be considered an adventure sport. Back then, people let storms do the chasing and took to their cellars when they heard a roaring wind.

Minnie Tims Harper lived with her husband and three children on a ranch eight miles from Childress. Recalling what happened one spring day decades after the fact, she described their ranch as being on "a lonely hilltop." Her husband often had to be gone for days at a time, making that hilltop "depressingly lonely."

That's why she welcomed any opportunity to hitch up the team, load the kids in the family buggy and go to Childress for supplies or simply to

A gutsy rancher's wife outran a storm in the family buggy. *Author's collection.*

visit friends. But one day she came close to paying a dear price for the sake of having someone to talk to. "I had imprudently visited too long…and had been too late starting home," she recalled in 1944.

Not only was it getting late in the day considering the distance she had to travel, but also, of her two horses, a fine-blooded single-footer named Walter had a fractious disposition. Beyond having to deal with him, she knew she'd have to stop to open and close three ranch gates along the way. It would be after dark before she and the kids got home.

She'd gone only a short distance from town when the wind picked up, and she noticed that "the atmosphere had grown hazy." Looking behind her, she saw a dark cloud building, though low on the horizon.

"I drove on unmindful of danger and was past the last house on my route before I thought again of the cloud," she wrote. "When I looked, I was alarmed. It was a wind cloud and moving swiftly toward us."

In modern meteorological speak, "wind cloud" likely means wall cloud, the dangerous formation from which tornados are spun. Indeed, the storm was already producing strong straight-line gusts. Tumbleweeds shot past the buggy, and blowing sand stung the back of Minnie's neck.

Turning back around in the buggy seat, she swatted the horses with her whip, the equivalent of stepping on the gas. The steady horse, Dixie, responded by picking up his gait. Walter bolted forward too fast, forcing Dixie to increase his pace just to keep up.

"I [envisioned] at once the team racing wildly across the prairie hitting prairie dog mounds, cat-claw bushes and thorny mesquite, dashing the children out one by one, or the team likely crashing into a barbed wire fence leaving our mangled bodies and buggy wreckage entangled in the wire," she wrote.

On the other hand, a mean storm churned in her direction as her buggy bounced over the unbroken prairie.

Moving as far forward in the seat as she could and bracing her feet against the dash, Minnie pulled the reins tight with both hands to slow the team while fighting an urge to make the horses go even faster.

"I was reasoning that if the storm did overtake us, the result might be just as fatal," she continued. "I could not, in either case, hope to save all the children. I even caught myself wondering which one I should try first to save. A maddening thought—there was no choice."

Suddenly, the wind stopped, followed by what Minnie described as a "brooding calm"—another sign that the looming storm cloud was about to drop a cyclone.

Clearly, the horses had picked up on Minnie's nervousness, as had her children. The kids became "cross and fretful," while the fractious horse tossed his head, shied at seemingly nothing and moved at an irregular gait. Watching every move the horses made, Minnie pushed them as fast as she thought reasonably safe. But the storm was getting closer.

Reaching the first gate, she pulled the horses to a stop, hopped out of the buggy, tied the reins to a fencepost and ran to open the gate. Then she had to unhitch, get back in the buggy, walk the team through, tie the horses again, climb down, close the gate and untie the horses.

"This same amount of precious time had to be wasted at each gate," she wrote. "After each ordeal, delayed by my clumsy shaking fingers, my nerves were keyed to the breaking point as I started on."

All the while, she planned how she'd get the children out of the buggy and into their storm cellar as soon as they got home, assuming they did. First, with the help of her oldest son, she'd get the children in the cellar. Then she'd unhitch the team so they'd have a fighting chance at survival.

Now within a quarter mile of their white, two-story ranch house, Minnie reined the team to open their gate.

"The wind was so strong that when I took two steps forward I was blown back one," she recalled.

When she got back on the buggy, the horses panicked. Chomping down on their bits with their heads up and ears forward, Dixie and Walter broke into a full gallop heading straight toward the strong plank fence around their yard.

"God help us!" Minnie screamed, pulling on the reins as hard as she could while trying to talk soothingly to the horses. When they paid no attention,

Minnie resorted to punishment, sawing the bits back and forth in their mouths. But still they ran, now galloping toward the sturdy corner post of the fence.

And then the storm hit with full force, ripping Minnie's hat from her head and streaming her long hair in front of her face, virtually blinding her. Above the screaming of her children, she heard a roaring sound.

"Grown vicious with fear for the children's safety, I jerked savagely at the right rein while damning the horses for unruly beasts," she wrote. "This treatment swung them enough to avoid disaster."

Walter was trying to get to the barn, but Dixie took control and pulled the buggy to its usual parking spot under a big cottonwood tree at their back gate. Still, Walter reared and plunged, his forefeet flattening an assortment of cans and buckets the wind had blown against the fence.

As limbs snapped from the trees and became deadly projectiles in the wind, Minnie managed to get Dixie's reins tied to the fence. When Walter pulled his reins from her hands, she decided she had done all she could for the horses. Grabbing her baby from her oldest son, the tenacious ranch wife half led, half dragged her two boys to the safety of the cellar.

Her written account stops suddenly there. But no matter how much damage the storm ended up doing to her home, she and her children survived her wild race against the wind.

DUSTERS

Eighty-five years old, Mary Jane Weaver told her daughter-in-law her life story back in 1940. Born six years before the Civil War, she had seen a lot during that long lifetime. But what happened one spring afternoon in Vega, the seat of Oldham County, ranked high on her list of the most memorable.

As she recalled it, she had been visiting at her brother Rufus's residence. He was outside, in the fashion of old-time Texans, sitting on the porch. She was inside when he called for her to join him.

"I just wanted you to see what was comin'," he said, pointing toward a towering, billowing blackness headed in their direction.

It looked like a monstrous thunderstorm, minus any lightning, thunder or the refreshing smell of distant rain.

"We all believed it was a cyclone," Mrs. Weaver recalled. "It was just rollin' and boilin'. In less than ten minutes, it was just as dark as any night you ever saw."

Back inside the house, she discovered that she literally could not see her hand before her face. The sun-killing phenomenon descending on the Panhandle that day was not a tornado. It was a dust storm.

"About that time I heard a train whistle," she continued. "The train went within twenty feet of Rufus's house, and the headlight just give out a little glow, not a bit bigger than the top of a teacup."

The air was so full of dirt that Mrs. Weaver and her brother had trouble breathing. That eased once the storm passed, but the next morning, everything in the house bore a coating of fine dust.

In telling her daughter-in-law about the storm that turned day into night, Mrs. Weaver didn't mention a date, but it probably was the storm that swept across the Panhandle on April 14, 1935—Palm Sunday.

An earlier storm on March 3 had been more severe, but it had blown through at night. The Palm Sunday storm was the second worst of 350 dust storms recorded from 1932 to 1937. In time, people dropped "Palm" in describing the event and started referring to that day as Black Sunday.

When the storm hit Stinnett, in Hutchinson County northeast of Amarillo, Mrs. Weaver's daughter Myrtle was about to serve dinner (as Texans then commonly called the noon meal) in the café she and her husband operated.

"Somebody come runnin' to the café and told her to go to the courthouse and get there quick," Mrs. Weaver said.

Myrtle ran back into the kitchen, covered the food and grabbed her son. Her waitress collected Myrtle's daughter, and they ran to the courthouse. By the time they got inside the fence that surrounded the building, it was too dark to see. And then Myrtle dropped her son.

"The dust was so thick she couldn't find him," Myrtle's mother continued. "But he cried out and she grabbed him by his hair."

Later that afternoon, the same storm raced through nearby Amarillo at fifty miles per hour.

"We thought the world was coming to an end," Dessie M. Hanburry recalled a half century later. "It was so dark you couldn't see the light in the room. I've never witnessed darkness so dark."

Artist Alexandre Hogue grew up in Texas and also experienced the dust storms of the 1930s.

"I saw lush grazing land turn into sand dunes," he later recalled. "Thistles blew in, and fences would be covered in just a few hours. Railroads had plows fighting it just like they fought snow."

A painting inspired by those storms and their aftermath, the 1933 *Dust Bowl*, hangs in the National Museum of American Art at the Smithsonian

Black Sunday in Perryton, April 14, 1935. *XIT Ranch Museum, Dalhart.*

Institution in Washington. "To me, as an artist," Hogue went on, "[the dusters were] beautiful in a terrifying way. I painted it for that terrifying beauty."

Black Sunday brought a new term to the American lexicon, though its creation had not been intentional. Reporting on the terrible, multistate storm, Associated Press writer Robert Geiger had written this sentence: "Three little words, achingly familiar on a Western farmer's tongue, rule life in the dust bowl of the continent—if it rains." The term caught on. Not "if it rains," but "dust bowl," which rapidly became Dust Bowl.

When the drought finally broke and the High Plains greened up again, Dalhart newspaper editor John L. McCarty, who throughout the windstorm-whipped dry spell had been using his bully pulpit to put as pretty a face as he could on the bleak economic and environmental conditions in his part of the Panhandle, offered a fifty-dollar cash reward for the name of anyone who had used the term "Dust Bowl" prior to April 25, 1935. Other newspapers picked up on the story. "The Texan…offers to pay the coiner's round-trip fare to Dalhart, take him on a tour of the old dust bowl area where now records in crop, grass and fat cattle are being established, and then honor him with a banquet," the Amarillo newspaper noted.

Whether anyone collected the reward seems to have gone unreported, but the fifty dollars likely went unpaid unless McCarty offered it to Geiger.

The wind still blows dust in the Panhandle, but soil conservation efforts begun following the Depression keep most of the dirt where it belongs—on the ground.

WORLD'S TALLEST WINDMILL NO MORE

In 1887, the Panhandle and much of the rest of Texas suffered from one of the worst droughts in the state's known history.

On the giant XIT, land the state had traded to a group of investors to fund construction of a new capitol in Austin, ranch management faced a problem: too many cattle with too little ground water. To make matters worse, the ranch had more livestock on the way.

The water shortage had grown particularly acute on the southern end of the ranch in the Yellow House Division, the acreage intended to serve as

This replica of the old XIT Ranch windmill in Littlefield used to be world's tallest. *Photo by Mike Cox.*

the XIT's enormous breeding pasture. One of the seven (eventually eight) separately run ranches that made up the three-million-acre spread on the western edge of the Panhandle, Yellow House got its name because of its most striking geographic feature, known originally as El Canyon de Casa Amarillas. A South Plains landmark since first noted by Spanish explorers, the canyon stretched to the northwest of what is now Lubbock for thirty-five miles.

To provide enough water for the livestock expected on the Yellow House, ranch manager B.H. "Barbecue" Campbell contracted with two drillers to bring in water wells in the canyon. After a slow start, the men finally made two shallow wells with modest flows, but Campbell wanted artesian water.

Meanwhile, carpenters built wooden troughs that cowboys had to fill with buckets. That being highly inefficient, the division manager oversaw construction of an innovative horse-powered pump and a water distribution system that consisted of a series of wooden boxes moved by chain. Soon, several of those watered the growing number of cattle in the canyon, but they were still just a stopgap remedy until better wells pumped by windmills could be established.

A surveying crew continued looking for likely drilling sites, and a series of deep and shallow wells came in as the canyon began to sprout wooden windmills like so many sunflowers. Averaging thirty-four feet high, the towers supported wheels ranging from twelve to eighteen feet across.

But in the deeper end of the canyon, a thirty-four-foot windmill did not get enough wind to work efficiently. Pondering what to do, someone on the ranch's managerial side came up with the sensible idea of building a windmill tall enough to poke above the sides of the canyon so it could catch the generally more robust wind blowing across the open plains.

The result was a wooden windmill tower that rose 132 feet—the equivalent of a thirteen-story building—to support a wheel with 12-foot blades. When operable, it worked just fine, but the mill was so tall that the ranch had trouble finding a windmill man brave—or dumb—enough to climb to the top to grease it and perform other maintenance. Recruitment became even more difficult after one man fell to his death from the top of the giant mill.

The giant XIT windmill, one more superlative on a ranch with more than its share of big numbers, was only one of 325 mills the ranch had at the peak of its operation in 1900. Eighty of those stood on the Yellow House Division.

In the early 1900s, the XIT's owners—struggling for a return on investment they had yet to realize—decided to discontinue raising cattle. Their new business model would be to make back their money by breaking up the huge acreage the syndicate owned and selling smaller parcels as ranches or farms.

Drought ravaged the XIT when it first began operation in 1887, but as these cowboys in slickers could attest, sometimes it did rain on the huge Panhandle ranch. *XIT Ranch Museum, Dalhart, Texas.*

Austin-based cattleman George W. Littlefield bought the 312,175-acre Yellow House Division in the summer of 1901 for two dollars an acre and renamed it the Yellow House Ranch. In addition, he purchased five thousand cows and two hundred registered Hereford bulls from the XIT, placing them on his new holding.

Having done well in the cattle business and as a banker, in 1912 he signed a contract with the Santa Fe Railroad granting right of way across his land. Realizing the railroad would bring many more people to that part of the plains, he organized the Littlefield Land Co. the same year and set aside land for the Lamb County town that would bear his name.

The Yellow House Ranch, managed by Littlefield's nephew, continued in operation until Littlefield's death in 1920. Within a few years after that, the Littlefield estate sold off the rest of the land. Whether the giant windmill in the Yellow House canyon still functioned after nearly forty years is not known, but a windstorm on Thanksgiving Day 1926 turned it into so much scrap lumber.

Forty-one years passed before someone suggested to the Littlefield Chamber of Commerce in 1967 that it should think about building a replica of the old XIT giant as a tourist attraction. Agreeing that was a good idea, chamber members and staff came up with the necessary money and got the Santa Fe Railroad to donate enough land near its depot at State Highway 84 and XIT Avenue (known as Delano Street at the time) to accommodate the tower. A longtime windmill man named Buck Ross headed the crew that put together the new tower and raised it into place on May 27, 1969.

Unlike its historic predecessor, the new tower was made of steel and stood only 114 feet. Even with a 12-foot wheel on top, it lacked 6 feet compared to the original. Nevertheless, the Littlefield chamber proclaimed it the world's tallest windmill and began touting it as a must-see for visitors. A year later, the Texas Historical Commission placed a historical marker at the site.

Unfortunately for boosters of Littlefield, despite what the town's promotional material says, it no longer can claim that it has the world's tallest windmill. Alas, the Lamb County seat can't even brag that it has Texas's tallest windmill. That distinction now belongs to a collection of towering wind turbines outside Snyder in Scurry County. Generating three megawatts of power each, they rise 345 feet.

The towers weren't built with any intent to best Littlefield's big windmill. Just as was the case with the original XIT giant, it's all about reaching for the prevailing wind. The Snyder towers were built high so that the three huge blades each of them supports would be at the elevation where the wind in that area is strongest.

Ghost Towns

Tee Pee City

A buffalo wasn't the only critter that could get skinned on the High Plains if he wasn't careful.

In 1877, when the Panhandle still teemed with hundreds of thousands of shaggy-haired bison, a young traveling salesman checked in with his home office at Galveston by telegraph from Henrietta. He worked for Leon and H. Blum, then the Southwest's largest wholesaler of staple and dry goods

"They directed me to proceed to Tee Pee City in Motley County to collect an account against Armstrong, who operated a general store [there]," the onetime salesman later recalled.

Founded in 1875 as a buffalo hunter camp on the site of an old Comanche village on the east side of Tee Pee Creek, where it enters the middle fork of the Pease River, Tee Pee City was one of the Panhandle's first settlements. Consisting of dugouts, tents and a few frame buildings, it boasted a couple saloons, a small hotel and one or two eating places not quite refined enough to be called restaurants. In addition to booze, the saloons offered girls and gambling. Finally, Tee Pee City had one or two retail establishments, including the store operated by Isaac O. Armstrong, the fellow whose account stood in arrears.

Armstrong and his partner reported to Charles Rath and Lee Reynolds, traders who had hauled everything it took to start Tee Pee City from Dodge City, Kansas. Rath and Reynolds had since moved on to the Clear Fork of the Brazos, where they had opened another buffalo hunter trading post.

Knowing that nothing lay between Henrietta and Tee Pee City but open prairie, the salesman got a horse and a packhorse and rode northwest for 170 miles or so until he found the place.

"When I reached Tee Pee City," the salesman continued, "I found Armstrong had gone to Liberal, Kansas, with a load of buffalo hides and to bring back merchandise. The smallpox was raging in the town, many people suffering from the epidemic. I went down the creek about a mile and established my camp and waited."

Three or four days later, Armstrong returned from his buying trip, and the salesman hit him up about "the matter of settlement."

Lacking any ready cash but having a small mountain of unsold buffalo hides on his hands, Anderson cleverly—he thought—offered to pay off what he owed in hides. Unfortunately, Anderson didn't know what the salesman knew. Before leaving Henrietta, thanks to the telegraph, he had learned of a recent "sensational rise in the price of buffalo hides."

Realizing the hides in question would fetch a lot more than Anderson thought, the salesman readily agreed to the merchant's proposition. In fact, he later said, "I bought all the hides he had…gave him credit for the account he owed and wrote a draft on the house [the Galveston jobber he represented] for the difference."

The young salesman then chartered every available wagon in Tee Pee City, all seven or eight of them, loaded them with the newly purchased hides and headed east for the nearest market in Fort Worth. Hurrying back to Henrietta from the community that would later be known as Cowtown, the salesman wired his company about the draft he'd written.

"In the deal I made several hundred dollars for my employers," he said.

Barely a year later, most of the buffalo had been killed or moved off, and Tee Pee City declined, though Armstrong continued to run his store until his death in 1884. Tee Pee City got a second wind when ranching came to the South Plains as merchants realized cowboys could spend as freely on booze and dance hall girls as the buffalo hunters had.

Rowdy cowboys kept the Texas Rangers busy and greatly annoyed the pious owners of the sprawling Matador Ranch. When it got the opportunity in 1904, the ranch gladly bought the land on which Tee Pee City stood and quickly killed off the town.

The salesman who had skinned Anderson in the financial sense was Sam Lazarus, a man who continued to demonstrate his business acumen. Lazarus, who by then lived in St. Louis, told the Tee Pee City story to G.E. Hamilton in 1921 on board his private railroad car between Quanah and

Roaring Springs. Hamilton related the story to the editor of the *Matador Tribune*, who published it. The reason Lazarus had his own railroad car was because he was president of the Quanah, Acme and Pacific Railroad.

The only reminders of Tee Pee City today are a gray granite historical marker put up by the state in 1936 on a mesa just west of the site, Anderson's grave and the graves of two children.

A Letter from Estacado

On May 2, 1887, someone living in Crosby County who used only the initials R.P.S. wrote a letter to the editor of the *Austin Daily Statesman*.

"How many readers of this article, who were school boys and girls twenty-five or thirty years ago, remember being taught that the Llano Estacado was a great sandy plain, whose dreary wastes stretched from the interior of New Mexico down into Texas, and, as far south as Mitchell and Taylor counties are now located?" the author began.

Actually, the writer continued, the notion that the Llano Estacado consisted of nothing but desert was only a myth. In reality, the region was a "great, grassy plateau, whose southern edge crosses the lower parts of Lubbock, Crosby and Dickens counties."

R.P.S., whoever he or she was, lived in Estacado. The town, among the older communities on the South Plains, had been founded in 1879 by Paris Cox, a Quaker from Indiana. Envisioning a colony of fellow members of the friendly persuasion, he had named the place Marietta for his wife, Mary, but when a post office was opened there in 1884, the community was renamed Estacado. In 1886, it became the seat of government for newly established Crosby County, but the railroad missed it, the county seat got moved to Crosbyton and Estacado in time became a ghost town.

The term "caprock" had not yet been used to describe the sudden increase in elevation that marks the southern edge of the High Plains, but the anonymous writer painted a word picture demonstrating strong powers of observation:

> *As the traveler approaches the plains he sees its whole outline towering up before him, appearing like a mountain chain, without the appearance of peaks. Upon a nearer approach he finds what appeared to be mountains is a tall precipitous cliff, 200 to 300 feet high, stretching as far as the eye can see, from right to left, with a smooth, even top. At intervals a gorge cuts its*

way into the plain, only for a short distance, to end in the same precipitous manner as the outside cliffs.

With "great labor," the writer continued, a traveler reaches the plains above, "a great, smooth, grassy plateau bringing to mind that perhaps here the creator of the universe had, at the creation, laid out a vast parade ground upon which to marshal the armies of Heaven."

After devoting a few paragraphs to playa lakes and mirages, their opposite, the author waxes on for a couple more paragraphs about the beauty of High Plains sunsets.

Having covered the topography of the Llano Estacado, the writer turned to its fauna: pronghorn antelope, black bear, deer, turkey, quail, cougar, wolf and bobcat. Finally, the writer ends the report with a riff on skunks.

"The skunk is the scourge of the plains," the anonymous correspondent wrote. "There are two varieties—the large striped skunk and the small black one. The small black skunk the cowboy fears more than he does the rattlesnake."

It's hard to imagine a polecat trumping an angry buzztail when it came to a cowpoke's fear factor, but a skunk could sure stink up a place or person—and sometimes they carried rabies.

"Crawling around at night it [the dreaded skunk] frequently finds its way into a camp, when, without warning, it attacks the sleeping camper, inflicting wounds upon the face and hands that have occasionally proven fatal," the writer warned.

Indeed, back then no effective treatment existed for those who became infected with the rabies virus. And hydrophobia, as it was then known, was not an easy death.

The letter writer went on to report that only a few days earlier, two young boys sleeping on the floor were bitten by a skunk. "Their cries brought their father into the room, when he too was bitten." That a skunk would venture into a house occupied by humans is a sign it could be rabid.

"The father and two sons were taken south of here," the letter continued, "hunting for a madstone, and it is to be hoped they will be saved from hydrophobic death."

Rather, it was to be hoped that they didn't have rabies because a madstone would have done them no good. If they had rabies, the Panhandle would soon have three fresh graves.

Next, the writer turned his attention to the Panhandle cowboy, "that class of society so unjustly treated by ignorant writers.

"The cowboy following his daily avocation, riding broncos or following in the wake of the wild stampede, cannot be judged by the world's standards of a gentleman," the anonymous writer went on. "On an intimate acquaintance with them, one finds that true manhood can and does exist under so wild an exterior."

To support that, the writer told a story illustrating "the courage and quick perception of the cowboy when in danger."

Seeing an approaching thunderstorm on the horizon, an outfit on a roundup put up a small tent when it made camp for the night.

"During the night a rattlesnake made its presence known among the sleeping cowboys," the correspondent wrote. "Immediately there was a rush, each one making an exit for himself with his knife through the sides of the tent."

In the rush to escape, one of the cowboys stepped on the snake.

"He quickly concluded that because it had not struck him, and that so much of its body was squirming around his legs, that he must be standing on it near its head."

Not being able to see whether he had guessed correctly, he just stood there listening to the agitating rattling of the reptile until his fellow cowboys tore away the tent and killed the intruder.

"I leave it to my readers to determine if one who would thus risk his own life to save that of his companions can be the villain the cowboy is so often portrayed," the writer concluded.

MORE THAN NAMES ON THE MAP

BOOKER

The Lipscomb County town of Booker actually started out as LaKemp, Oklahoma, but as the saying goes, it got to Texas as soon as it could.

One of Texas's northernmost communities, Booker lies only three miles south of the Texas-Oklahoma border at the top of the Panhandle, but that's seven miles farther south than it used to be when it was in Beaver County, Oklahoma. The change of address had nothing to do with its residents wanting to be Texans, however. They just wanted to live somewhere with a more promising future, no matter the location of their capital. And back then, a town's prosperity had a lot to do with whether it enjoyed railroad service.

Primarily on the belief that when the Santa Fe Railroad built a line from Shattuck, Oklahoma, across the northern Panhandle, the rails would cut through newly organized Beaver County, developers platted a town site in 1909. The new town in the new state (Oklahoma had only gained statehood two years before) would be named for David L. Kemp, but when the application for a new post office hit Washington, the Post Office Department notified the town site promoters that Oklahoma already had a Kemp City. So someone dressed up "Kemp" with a fancy-looking "La" and made it LaKemp.

In addition to its new post office, LaKemp soon boasted a hotel, a boardinghouse, a general store, a bank, a café (albeit one in a tent), a barbershop, a blacksmith shop, a lumberyard, a livery stable, a drugstore and other businesses. Within a year, the new town had its own newspaper, the *LaKemp Mirror*.

For the next eight years, LaKemp enjoyed relative prosperity as a business center for farmers and ranchers, but when the Santa Fe finally began surveying its long-anticipated trackage eastward from Shattuck, it became apparent that the route would bypass LaKemp by considerably more than a country mile. In fact, the line would be built no nearer than seven miles from town.

Not that the Santa Fe opposed civic development. On August 2, 1917, railroad officials filed a plat with the Lipscomb County clerk for a new town site in Texas to be named Booker in honor of B.F. Booker, an early-day Santa Fe locating engineer. Additional residential lots were platted that December 10.

Earlier that year, however, the United States had entered the war between Great Britain and Germany. That forced the Santa Fe to shut down construction after the new line reached Follett, a community twenty-two miles west of the planned town of Booker. With the war's end in November 1918, work on the tracks resumed early in 1919, and the first train rolled into Booker on the Fourth of July that year.

Meanwhile, back in LaKemp, Oklahoma, most of its residents had already begun to move to Booker. They took their town with them, jacking up its frame houses and business buildings and hauling them by mule team to the new town site in Texas. Crossing the open prairie, ten mules could pull a two-room house complete with a brick chimney just fine. The town doctor, Ira T. Smith, and his wife had been the first to make the move.

Two brothers who had a real estate business in LaKemp, J.W. and O.C. Bell, were among the Okies who decided to become Texans. J.W. Bell served as LaKemp's postmaster, and he had already written to Washington asking permission to relocate the post office across the state line to the new town in Lipscomb County.

As he patiently waited for an answer, he saw postal volume and business in general drying up faster than a playa lake in a drought. Deciding he couldn't wait on Washington any longer, Bell hired a wagon and team and moved all the postal fixtures and supplies to Booker overnight. After handling mail in Booker for a full year, Bell finally got a letter from Washington approving the move.

By that time, LaKemp had become a ghost town. Booker, on the other hand, flourished until the Dust Bowl days of the 1930s. Oil play in the 1950s and 1960s perked up business, and contrary to the trend in many rural towns in Texas, Booker actually gained population from 2000 to 2010, growing to 1,516 from 1,315 residents.

The original Santa Fe Railroad depot in Booker, a town that got to Texas as soon as it could. *Author's collection.*

Ironically enough, that growth spurt came without rail service. The Santa Fe had discontinued passenger service to Booker in the 1950s. And in 2006, its corporate successor, the Burlington Northern Santa Fe, dropped rail service altogether.

At least someone in Booker took the community's small size and railroad's departure good-naturedly, putting up a large sign on the northern edge of town that reads, "Booker Next 9 Exits."

PUNKIN CENTER

An old Irish legend that must have come to Texas with some of its earliest settlers has grown into a profitable business for Lone Star farmers: cultivating a large variety of squash that sells by the ton every fall.

We're talking about pumpkins, of course. Or, to the Texas tongue, "punkins."

It's not too difficult to dig up the tale that transformed pumpkins into edible holiday icons, but there is an interesting puzzle of geographic nomenclature to consider: the Punkin Center phenomenon. If anyone ever tells you that they're from Punkin Center, better ask them to be more specific. Unique as that place name might seem, Texas has four different communities called Punkin Center.

Listed alphabetically, there's Punkin Center in Dawson County, Punkin Center in Eastland County, Punkin Center in Hardeman County and Punkin Center in Parker County. Oh, and in Wichita County, the community of Haynesville is locally known as Punkin Center, even though Haynesville is its official name.

Elsewhere across the United States, four other communities call themselves Punkin Center. But unlike Texas, which has to be bigger about everything, each of the non-Texas Punkin Centers is in a different state: Arizona, Kansas, Louisiana and Missouri.

Strange as the name Punkin Center may seem, according to the website www.placesnamed.com, Punkin Center is the 4,438th most popular town name in the United States. It also shows up on a website devoted to America's funniest town names, but that site lists Punkin Center, Kansas, not the Texas PCs.

Texas singer David Allen Coe sure likes the name. In 1976, he recorded a song called "The Punkin Center Barn Dance."

But here's the weird thing about Punkin Centers in Texas. None of them are in counties particularly known for their bounteous pumpkin crops.

Floyd County, which has an annual Punkin Festival but no community named Punkin Center, is the top pumpkin-producing county in Texas. Other prolific producers of pumpkins are the plains counties of Bailey, Hale, Lamb and Lubbock.

Texas A&M University says that Texas ranks in the top ten of pumpkin-producing states (but don't forget we're number one in terms of number of Punkin Centers). The estimated value of Texas's annual pumpkin harvest is $4.6 million, most of the pumpkins going for ornamental (read: Halloween) purposes.

And that brings us back to that old Irish folktale, without which Texas's pumpkin industry would have remained a mere pumpkin in metaphor, not a pretty economic carriage.

Back in the eighteenth century, an Irishman named Jack had an unfortunate, though not surprising, propensity for strong beverage. But he did not let his drinking get in the way of his antipathy toward the devil, whom he tricked into climbing an apple tree. Once Jack had the devil treed, he carved a cross on the tree's trunk, an action he knew would prevent the devil from climbing down. The devil pleaded for his freedom, and Jack finally struck a deal: if Jack let him down, the devil had to agree never to come after Jack's soul.

That seemed like a good trade to the devil, so Jack covered the cross, and Satan was free to return to his normal level of devilment. Unfortunately for Jack, when he made his deal with the devil, he forgot to write in an immortality clause. When Jack died, his hard drinking, penuriousness and other issues sent his spirit down instead of up.

The devil proved true to his word and refused to allow Jack into the nether regions. But Jack did not qualify for heaven either and sadly realized it would have been better not to barter with the devil. Unfortunately, his spirit was doomed to wander forever. It being dark out, the devil graciously threw a glowing coal at Jack so he could find his way around. Jack placed the red-hot coal in a hollowed turnip to make himself a lantern.

Somehow over the centuries, the turnip gave way to the pumpkin, hence the enduring symbol of Halloween, the jack-o'-lantern. All of this makes about as much sense as naming four different communities in the same state Punkin Center.

Earth

Why on earth would someone name a town Earth?

Just imagine the communication inconveniences plaguing those living in the Lamb County community of Earth.

"Where're you from?"

"I'm from Earth."

"Har, har! Me, too. Where are you really from?"

"I said I'm from Earth."

"Seriously, where are you from?"

When you live in this High Plains town some seventy miles northwest of Lubbock, every time you say goodbye to a visitor, you have to guard against a polite, "I'll look forward to seeing you the next time you come to Earth."

Or say you moved to Austin to attend the University of Texas but occasionally liked to go home to see family and friends.

"I'm going back to Earth for the holidays."

Even if you stayed behind, when you were ready to go someplace else, telling your friends, "I'm leaving Earth for a few days" could net a few snickers.

Obviously, simply asking someone if he had ever visited Earth could cause misunderstanding.

Rancher William E. Halsell did not make the heavens above or the fishes in the sea, but he created Earth in 1924. He had been in the area since 1901, when he bought up a huge chunk of the old XIT Ranch for two dollars an acre. In August 1924, he had a town site platted and began selling lots.

The Halsell Land Co. built a hotel, a cotton gin and the first house. Within a couple of years, Earth could boast a café, a service station, a store or two and more residences. And that's about all the solid ground there is when it comes to the history of Earth.

Researchers have unearthed at least four versions of how a point in a rural High Plains county came to be called Earth.

The first settlers wanted to call the new town Tulsa, but the U.S. Post Office quickly took them back to Tulsa as a bad choice since such a town already existed in Oklahoma.

Halsell supposedly called his town Fairlawn (some say Fairlene), but the frequent blowing dirt inspired someone to come up with Earth.

Another tale has R.C. "Daddy" Reeves, who operated the new town's hotel, declaring, "We've got more earth here than anything else; let's call it Earth."

A final version has Halsell, wanting to emphasize the fertile soil around his town, coming up with Good Earth. Washington, this tale holds, did away with "Good" and made the post office plain old Earth.

While accounts vary as to how Earth, Texas, got its worldly name, you can take to the soil bank that Earth is the only place in the United States called Earth. (There's Black Earth, Wisconsin; Blue Earth, Minnesota; White Earth, Minnesota, and Maryland; Earth City, Missouri; and Middle Earth, Maryland; but that's as close as it gets.) Neither does a global search reveal another Earth anywhere on Earth.

Someone seemingly with all the time on earth has also discovered that in addition to Earth, the state of Texas has a small solar system of other towns named after the planets swirling around our sun. Beyond Earth, Texas's extraterrestrial town names include Mercury, Mars, Saturn and Pluto. Several states have Venus, Jupiter and Neptune as town names, though no state has chosen to honor Uranus.

But to get back to Earth, despite its all-encompassing name, it's a pretty down-to-earth community, a rural agricultural center whose principal landmark is a shiny silver-colored water tower with the green (as in "God's green earth") letters E-A-R-T-H painted on its tank.

Speaking of paint, several of the buildings along State Highway 70, the town's main thoroughfare, have been enhanced by someone handy with a brush. The former movie theater, long since closed, has been dolled up as "The Tin Star," featuring Anthony Perkins perpetually playing in *The Blob*, with showings at 6:00 and 10:00 p.m. daily and matinees at 2:00 p.m. on Saturdays. Down the street at Main and Cedar is the paint-

A sign marking the city limits of Earth, Texas. *Photo by Mike Cox.*

enhanced office of the *Earth News,* an imaginary newspaper "dedicated to the Development of the World's Richest Irrigation Area." On the side of another building, someone painted a giant green population sign reading, "Earth Pop. 1019."

That population is not big enough to support its own school, so students go to class in nearby Springlake. Because of that, the football team is known as the Wolverines, not Earthmen.

Small but tough, Earth endured the Dust Bowl and the Depression but stayed in slow decline until the late 1970s. The high point of Earth's orbit came in 1980, when the town's population peaked at 1,512. But the number of those calling Earth home has dropped by nearly a third since then.

Even the Dairy Queen stands abandoned these days.

KENT COUNTY

Folks in Kent County on the upper reaches of the Salt and Double Mountain Forks of the Brazos River don't have to worry about crowded schools, waiting in line at restaurants and movie theaters or being stuck in traffic on congested roadways.

Only 808 people occupy 902.4 square miles of land in one of Texas's least-populated political subdivisions—slightly fewer than 1 person per square mile. That's a decline of 5.9 percent since the 2000 U.S. Census, when enumerators counted 859 folks in the county. Kent County does not have the smallest population of any Texas county—an honor that goes to Loving County, with 82 residents—but it's one of only a handful with fewer than 1,000 residents.

However, Kent County does have the distinction of having the newest county seat, and that's an interesting story.

The legislature created the county in 1876, but that was only putting a name on the map. (The county was named for Andrew Kent, one of the thirty-two men who rode from Gonzales to defend the Alamo after the siege had begun.) For judicial purposes, the new county was attached to Scurry County. By the late 1880s, area ranchers were getting tired of riding to Snyder to vote and pay their taxes, but not enough people were in the area to organize a county government until 1892, when Kent County's first commissioner's court had its first meeting under a large mesquite tree.

Beneath that mesquite, the new commissioners voted to call an election to determine where the county seat would be. The winning location was a point about two miles south of the tree, property that belonged to real estate speculator R.L. Rhomberg.

To his credit, Rhomberg did not opt to name the new town after himself, even though it would have been a mildly amusing play on words. Instead, he decided on Clairemont, after a young relative, Miss Claire Becker.

Thanks to cotton growing, ranching and eventually oil production, Kent County grew each decade until 1940. The year before World War II erupted, the county had 3,413 residents, its peak population. By 1950, old-timers in Clairemont began to realize that something that happened in 1907 had been more significant than they thought at the time: the railroad had bypassed Clairemont.

The little community of Jay Flat, however, had decided it would go to the railroad. The people pulled up stakes and relocated on the newly laid tracks, two miles from their original community. Three years later, in 1910, they incorporated as Jayton.

Neither Jayton nor Clairemont became big towns, but thanks to its rail connection, Jayton did better than Clairemont. In 1952, a lawsuit was filed challenging Clairemont's status as county seat. Two years later, the plaintiffs won, and Jayton became the new capital.

County seat wars were common in Texas during the late nineteenth and early twentieth centuries, but the fight in the early 1950s was the last time that any two Texas towns vied for that status.

Today, Clairemont is about as close to a ghost town as a place can get. Even so, the 2010 census listed 15 residents, the same number for 1990. On the other hand, the population of Jayton was 534 in 2010, an increase of 21 residents since the 2000 census. Maybe the boom is finally on.

CHARACTERS

MOBEETIE'S PARSON BROWN

In 1887, newly married John M. Barcus filled the pulpit of the Methodist church in Graham, then one of only a handful of towns in northwest Texas.

The twenty-seven-year-old, Arkansas-born preacher belonged to the Weatherford District of his denomination's Northwest Texas Conference. That district included all of the South Plains and the Panhandle, as well as a chunk of what is now Oklahoma.

That spring, the district's presiding elder, Jerome Haralson, asked Barcus to join him on a swing through the barely settled portion of his territory. He also recruited two other preachers for the trip.

On May 23, traveling in two hacks, the four clergymen left Graham. Fortunately for posterity, Barcus later set his experiences down in an article for the *Methodist Historical Quarterly* in 1909.

From Graham, they went to Seymour and then Vernon. After crossing the Red River into Greer County, Texas (given to Oklahoma by the U.S. Supreme Court in 1896), their next stop was Mangum, the county seat. After traveling across Indian Territory, they reached Mobeetie, the Panhandle's oldest community.

"We found about 500 people," Barcus wrote, "mostly from the North. The U.S. Army post [Fort Elliott] with about 200 soldiers was located here. Among the soldiers were a number of Indians used as scouts."

After setting up camp on Sweetwater Creek, Elder Haralson and one of the preachers left for an outlying camp meeting, leaving Barcus and the remaining preacher in Mobeetie.

The two preachers "wrote out some notices announcing preaching at night at the school house and tacked them up around town. The saloon men tore them down and got a boy with a cowbell to go around with a banner on which they had written: 'Haymakers in town! Come out to the school house tonight.'"

Thanks to the extra effort on the part of the whiskey sellers, nine people showed up.

Mobeetie eventually got its own Methodist church, and Barcus returned to his congregation in Graham before moving on to another in a long string of other churches. He and his wife had seven children who lived to adulthood, and one of them may have eventually moved to the Panhandle.

That's just a guess, based on the fact that in a collection of cow country tales published in 1950, a character identified as "Dad Barkus" tells a couple of fun tales about a Methodist circuit rider who lived in Mobeetie not long after Barcus and the other preachers had been there. It could be that the author misspelled "Barcus," or it might just be a coincidence.

Whatever the facts, "Dad" had a couple of good stories to tell. Both had to do with someone he called Parson Brown. (A book on Mobeetie doesn't mention any old-time Methodist preachers by that name, so Brown may not have been his real name.)

The preacher stood tall and thin, almost always wearing a black Prince Albert coat and a high hat. As "Dad" recalled, Brown could "preach funeral sermons that would take an outlaw right up to Saint Peter's gate. Don't reckon he ever said a harm[ful] word about anybody."

On top of that, the circuit rider had a good sense of humor.

Parson Brown's wife ran a boardinghouse in Mobeetie. One time when Brown returned after a horseback trip just in time for supper, he placed his long coat on the back of his chair and sat down to some home cooking. But then he remembered he hadn't washed his hands and got up to do that.

As soon as he was gone, the town barber, one of the boardinghouse residents, excused himself, saying he needed to go to his room. He got back downstairs before the parson had finished up in the washroom.

Standing with his back to the others, the barber placed something in the pockets of the preacher's coat. Then he returned to his place and was busy chowing down when the parson returned to the table.

When the parson pulled his coat off the chair to put it back on, he noticed that its pockets were bulging. Reaching inside, he pulled out a long red stocking, a deck of cards and a half pint of whiskey.

As soon as the boarders saw those decidedly un-ministerial objects coming from his pockets, they commenced razzing the preacher.

"Well, how much money did you win?" asked one.

"Why be selfish with that bottle?" asked another.

"So what's her name?" asked the third.

Fortunately, Mrs. Brown took the gag good-naturedly, as did her husband.

Long before Mobeetie had a chamber of commerce, Parson Brown decided the town might get some favorable publicity because of its water. The preacher believed it had curative powers.

One day, he filled a jug and announced that he intended to send it off to be analyzed. Placing the jug on his front porch, he said he would get it to the post office in time for the 2:00 p.m. mail.

The same boarder who had earlier stuffed the preacher's pockets with icons of earthly pleasure happened to be walking out of the boardinghouse when Brown made his pronouncement. Quickly formulating an idea, the barber hurried to the drugstore and made a purchase. Back at the boardinghouse well before 2:00 p.m., he poured out some of the water and emptied a small packet into the jug.

Brown shipped it off on schedule. When the report came back from the chemist, the preacher learned that the water was indeed medicinal. In fact, it would do wonders as a laxative.

PLAINS PIONEER CHARLIE SAIGLING

When Charlie Saigling first saw the Panhandle, there wasn't any cotton, or grain fields or "anything."

In 1909, already thirty-two years old, he had just been handed fourteen sections of land by his father, who got it for $4,000.

Saigling, born in Houston in 1876, came to Hale County from McKinney, where he had a hardware store and funeral home. Before coming to McKinney, he had operated a flour mill with his father in Plano.

"My father traded a lumber yard for it," Saigling recalled in a 1969 interview published in the *Lubbock Avalanche-Journal*.

Saigling spent his final years in the old Hilton Hotel in downtown Plainview. At ninety-three, he still got up every morning and drove to his holdings nine miles south of Hale Center.

Sitting in his room on the top floor of the eight-story hotel, gazing out at Plainview's grain elevators and the surrounding agricultural fields, he remembered a time when his part of Texas looked vastly different.

"The foreman came to town and got me in a hack," Saigling said of the day he first arrived.

Above: Many of the Panhandle's first settlers initially lived in dugouts, though the character in this postcard is a bit fanciful. *Author's collection.*

Left: Panhandle pioneer Charlie Saigling lived out his life in Plainview's old Hilton Hotel, his room looking out on miles of agricultural land that had been open prairie when he first saw it. *Author's collection.*

From Plainview, the buggy creaked along over the open prairie. Finally, reining in the team, the foreman announced they had arrived.

"Here we are," the ranch boss said.

Saigling looked around and noted one dugout, a windmill and a barbed-wire fence that stretched on for miles. His new property did not boast many improvements, but he had plenty of land to work with.

Visiting Lubbock hoping to buy some lumber for a ranch house, Saigling found that the still-small town could not accommodate his needs. The closest place he could buy lumber was the railroad town of Colorado City in Mitchell County.

"I had the lumber shipped to Canyon," he said, "then a man hauled it down to the ranch."

When the lumber arrived, Saigling built his ranch house, a structure that still stood six decades later.

"I lived in the dugout until the house was finished," he said.

When he moved in, he took the wooden roof off the dugout and moved it elsewhere on his property. It lasted for years, he said, and probably would have held up longer had it not been for a fire that burned off about a section of his land some years later

All pioneer ranchers had their problems, but most of Saigling's worries were of either the four-legged or climatic variety. "I never had any problems with rustlers," he said. "There were a mighty good bunch of people up here."

One of Saigling's biggest headaches was the storm of 1918—January 8 to be exact.

"It was a terrible storm," he remembered. "We had to cut the fences to let the cattle out. A banker from Abernathy ended up feeding my cattle, and I probably fed someone else's."

Snow piled up in high drifts against the fences, Saigling said. Many cattle froze. And the snow kept falling. Ice covered frozen livestock. Another animal would wander up to seek shelter and die on top of the first one.

"The snow was so deep we could ride right over the fences and dead cattle," he said.

In another storm Saigling weathered, a freighting outfit on its way south to Lubbock got snowed in.

"They just sold groceries out of the wagons while they were there," he said. "Sure beat riding to town."

Most of the time, Saigling concentrated on the cattle business. But once he decided to delve into another enterprise: mule raising.

"I had a world of mules," he recalled. "I think I bought 225 head from a man named Bill Elwood. But I didn't make any money off 'em. I had to trade the mules for a section of land."

Five years after sharing some of his recollections with a young reporter, Saigling died on April 8, 1974, at ninety-eight years old.

PANHANDLE LAWMAKER ENVISIONED HIGH PLAINS STATEHOOD

Of the fifty states, only one—Washington—is named after a president.

But if a state senator from Hall County had gotten his bill through the legislature in 1915, the Panhandle and much of the rest of West Texas would have become a separate state named for Thomas Jefferson. Abilene would have been the capital of what would have become the forty-ninth state of the union. Though the political amputation would have ended Texas's status as the nation's largest state, both Jefferson and "Old" Texas still would have been bigger than all but a few of the other states.

Fanciful as that sounds, it would have been legal. That's because the joint resolution passed by Congress on March 1, 1845, provided that the new state of Texas, formerly an independent republic, could divide itself into as many as four other states. Any of them would automatically be entitled to admission to the Union.

Senator W.A. Johnson's bill to create the state of Jefferson, however, wasn't grounded on a desire to add to the recogition of the nation's third president. What it did have to do with was politics—more particularly, realizing better representation for West Texas in Congress.

The proposed state of Jefferson would have included four congressional districts and four state senatorial districts. Its eastern border would have been the western boundaries of, from north to south, Clay, Jack, Palo Pinto, Erath, Comanche, Mills, San Saba, Llano, Gillespie, Kimble, Edwards, Kinney and Maverick Counties.

"Senator Johnson contends that the western sections of the state have been unlawfully restrained from their lawful representatives in the Texas senate and national congress by the constant and persistent refusal of the legislature to redistrict," one newspaper reported on January 29, 1915, the day after Johnson put his bill in the hopper.

The lawmaker from Memphis, where he owned and edited the *Hall County Herald*, argued that the state's "liquor interests" had succeeded in blocking redistricting "by subscribing giant slush funds to control the politics of the state."

The legislature actually did have a redistricting bill before it, but Johnson must have believed it had no chance of passing. His proposal to create a new state had originally been looked on as a joke, but on January 31 the *San Antonio Light* said, in so many words, that the measure seemed to be growing legs.

"The phenomenal growth of West Texas and the development of antagonistic interests" made statehood for that area a necessity, Johnson argued.

The Alamo City newspaper continued, "A number of prominent antis [as in anti-liquor] in the state are said to be looking with favor on the proposition on account of the fact that a large part of the territory proposed to be included in the new state is hopelessly dry."

One place in the state not under the control of prohibitionists was the island city of Galveston, where beer and liquor flowed as freely as the daily Gulf tides.

Senator William L. Hall of Wharton County, whose district included Galveston, introduced on February 4 a resolution that would divide Texas into three states: the state of Jefferson as envisioned by his honorable colleague from Memphis, as well as North Texas and South Texas. Austin

Senator W.A. Johnson wanted the Panhandle to be a separate state named in honor of Thomas Jefferson. *Author's collection.*

would remain the capital of South Texas, while Palestine would become the seat of government for the state of North Texas.

The governor and lieutenant governor of "Old" Texas would continue in office as the chief executives of South Texas, but the new state would have to appoint two new U.S. senators. North Texas, on the other hand, would be represented by the current U.S. senators from Texas but would have to elect a governor and lieutenant governor. Jefferson, finally, would have to select all four positions.

The *Fort Worth Star-Telegram*, which under the Panhandle lawmaker's plan would be published in the state of North Texas, started printing a blank ballot every day so readers could mark it "For" or "Against" on the statehood issue and then mail it to the newspaper. Despite the Fort Worth newspaper's let's-see-what-the-people-think stance, the *Abilene Reporter* readily endorsed Johnson's plan. While agreeing that Texas was too big a state to remain undivided, the newspaper predicted it would be years before division happened. Another West Texas newspaper, the *Stamford Leader*, correctly noted that the notion of dividing Texas had been kicked around for half a century and likely would never happen.

On February 6, by a vote of four to two, the Senate Judiciary Committee favorably reported Johnson's bill, clearing the way for its consideration by the full Senate. Senator Hall, meanwhile, withdrew his resolution to divide Texas into three states but said he would bring it up again on the floor.

A savvy politician, Johnson knew his Panhandle statehood proposal had no realistic chance of passage. Indeed, by mid-session, it had become clear that Texas would remain undivided at least until the next session. But by 1917, Johnson and his colleagues were busy working to impeach and then remove Governor Jim Ferguson from office, and the question of carving up Texas got shoved way back on the political burner.

The idea of Panhandle statehood did not come up again until 1921, when Governor Pat Neff vetoed a bill that would have given West Texas its first agricultural and mechanical college. Once more, but this time with more vitriol than good humor, people in that part of the state began clamoring for statehood. The movement played out four years later when the legislature approved the creation of Texas Technological College at Lubbock.

Several times since the 1920s, a legislator has brought up the old notion of cutting up Texas, most recently in 1975, but doing so has long since been considered a political impossibility even if allowable under the law.

While Texas is the only state that retained the right to subdivide itself, its politicians were not the first to propose a state named after Thomas Jefferson.

It happened the first time in the Kansas Territory in 1859, when a group of citizens drafted a constitution for a territory named for the third president that included all of present Colorado and much of the area to the north, east and west. But Congress never recognized it and ended its unofficial existence in 1862 with the formal creation of the Territory of Colorado.

Following the Texas attempt to create a state of Jefferson midway into the second decade of the twentieth century, a final movement in 1941 to organize a state of Jefferson in northern California and southern Oregon died with the Japanese attack on Pearl Harbor that December 7.

As for the lawmaker who had first proposed turning part of Texas into a separate state honoring Jefferson, the Hall County newspaper editor won election as lieutenant governor in 1919. He served one term, dying in Memphis in 1923.

Indian Jim

Barely fifty years after the U.S. Cavalry forced the last hostile Indians out of the Panhandle, an Indian from New York made page-one news in Pampa and across the nation.

His name was James Garfield Brown, but he was much better known as simply "Indian Jim." Born in the 1880s (the exact date has not been determined) on the Oneida Reservation in central New York State, Jim stood six-foot-one and weighed 180 pounds. Educated at the Carlisle Indian School in Pennsylvania and Ontario Agricultural College, he had been a standout football player—strong and fast. Incredibly fast.

Like Jim Thorp, Brown could have become a professional athlete, but that didn't pay much in those days. Instead, he turned to the building trades, eventually specializing in laying paving bricks. With a muscle memory that must have been off the charts, he evolved into a human brick-laying machine who began attracting attention wherever he went.

Oil is what brought him to the High Plains. The petroleum boom that started in Hutchinson County and led to the development of the new town of Borger quickly spread twenty-eight miles southeast to Pampa, which had started when the Santa Fe Railroad came through the Panhandle in 1888. By the spring of 1927, the Gray County seat, fueled by the burgeoning Panhandle oil industry, was transforming itself from town to city. And that meant paved streets.

"Bricks Fly As 'Indian Jim' Brown Loafs With 33,000," the *Pampa Daily News* noted on April 29, 1927, as the city's streets were being paved with

Ripley's Believe It or Not! featured Indian Jim Brown in 1939. *Author's collection.*

heavy red bricks shipped in by rail from Kansas and Mineral Wells in Texas. According to the front-page story, Brown "placed more than 33,000 bricks in less than 8 hours and did not seem to be hurrying. Twelve men could not keep him supplied with bricks."

City engineer A.H. Doucette timed the Indian, finding he averaged placing three bricks per second. If he kept that up for eight hours, the engineer calculated, the total would be eighty thousand bricks. That pace would break Brown's own world record set on a job in Olathe, Kansas, when on September 12, 1926, he put down 64,644 paving bricks in seven hours and forty-eight minutes.

Prior to that spring, now-bustling Pampa had not had a single paved street. But on March 3, the Wichita Falls–based Stuckey Construction Co. began a project to get Pampa "out of the mud." By that November, twenty-four and a half city blocks extending along eleven streets had been paved with bricks, the bulk of the work accomplished by one man: "Indian Jim" Brown.

When the *Pampa Daily News* came out with a special "Paving Edition" on November 13, it ran a photograph of a big-hatted Brown in a typical pose setting three-inch bricks in wet concrete. "'Indian Jim' Brown, world's champion bricklayer, quickly and efficiently covered the concrete base on Pampa's wide streets. He was very intersting to watch," the caption read.

So who was Indian Jim?

Twelve years later, newspapers around the nation carried a *Ripley's Believe It Or Not!* cartoon featuring a drawing of Brown noting that "Indian Jim Brown—full blooded Oneida Indian—lays 58,000 paving bricks a day—207 tons…This is his daily average. He challenges any man."

Despite all the publicity he garnered, perhaps because he was Native American, newspapers did not dig particularly deep into his background. When he went to work for Stuckey is not known. Neither does there seem to be any information on whether he had a family, though there is some indication that he suffered from alcoholism.

What is known is that by the time he came to Pampa, Brown had been laying bricks for at least six years. In the summer of 1921, research shows he had helped pave the streets of Goodland, Kansas.

There, with six men using metal tongs constantly bringing him bricks (which weighed nine pounds each), Brown could lay 125 to 150 bricks a minute. He did the work leaning over from a standing position. Wearing leather pads to protect his hands, he placed bricks ambidextoursly at a pace of two to three bricks a second.

"His back seemed never to tire as he stooped over the smooth sand cushion and dropped bricks with monotonous regularity," one newspaper observed.

Brown left Pampa after laying nearly one million bricks. More than eighty years later, many of them are still there.

Technology is what finally proved faster than Indian Jim. By the early 1930s, though brick paving had been the industry standard since the turn

Indian Jim Brown put down the brick streets around the Gray County Courthouse in Pampa. *Author's collection.*

of the century, concrete had proven to be less labor-intensive, easier to spread and cheaper.

By the time the drawing of Brown appeared in *Ripley's Believe It Or Not!*, the use of brick paving was well past its prime. And so was Brown, his body doubtless beginning to show signs of wear after working—and drinking—as hard as he did.

What became of him is not known. The October 1, 1953 edition of the *Ukiah* [California] *News* notes that on Sunday, September 27, "Rev. DeFord took an aged Indian, Jim Brown, to the hospital." Whether that was the former champion bricklayer is not known, but an online search of thousands of digitized newspapers reveals no further mention of Indian Jim.

Gene Autry Comes to Childress

In the spring of 1938, a cowboy on the dodge rode into the Panhandle railroad town of Childress.

A little short on cash, he approached Rufus Layton, manager of the Palace Theater, about doing some work for him. Layton jumped at the opportunity, offering him a healthy amount of money for Depression times: $100.

For that kind of money, this cowboy wouldn't be taking tickets or sweeping up stale popcorn. He'd be singing, playing guitar and smiling big. Layton must have been smiling big, too, because the cowboy's name was Gene Autry. *The* Gene Autry.

Born to a farming family in 1907 in the East Texas town of Tioga, Autry learned to walk and ride a horse at about the same time. His grandfather was a Baptist preacher, and the youngster became a mainstay in the church choir. When he was a little older, he also got to be a good hand with a five-dollar mail-order guitar. His family moved to Ravia, Oklahoma, when he was fifteen. After graduating from high school there in 1925, he started working as a railroad telegrapher for the Frisco Line.

When the wire wasn't singing, Autry was. That's what he was doing when Will Rogers heard him and urged him to give up key-clicking for yodeling and strumming. Within a few years, Autry started singing on radio station KVOO in Tulsa. From there, he went to WLS in Chicago, where he performed on a show called *National Barn Dance*.

By 1932, he had written his first hit, "That Silver Haired Daddy of Mine." Two years later, he appeared in his first movie. Three years after that, in 1937, he had become the nation's top cowboy movie star. The cowboy crooner received eighty thousand fan letters a month, mostly from kids.

Why Autry happened to come to in Childress in 1938 did not get much attention, though plenty of people bought tickets for the Palace's showing of *Battle of Broadway* to see Autry "on stage in person."

Popular though he was, as the *Childress Index* noted, the singing cowboy had been having contract negotiation difficulties with his studio. To underscore his position, Autry disappeared from Hollywood, eventually showing up in Childress.

Why Childress? Maybe he was just passing through on his way to visit family and friends in Oklahoma. But back then Childress was a hopping place. It was no Fort Worth or Amarillo, but since the early 1900s it had been a division point on the Fort Worth and Denver Railroad, with a large yard employing a lot of people. Could be Autry had a friend in Childress from his days as a telegrapher.

Whether Autry came to town on the train or drove was not reported, but he stayed for a couple weeks, likely rooming at Hotel Childress, which now stands empty in downtown. Also unreported was whether he came to Childress with Champion, "The World's Wonder Horse."

But Autry earned his $100, putting on performances that doubtless featured one of his more recent hits, "Tumbling Tumbleweeds." Maybe he

Gene Autry hit Childress short of cash in 1938. *Author's collection.*

tried out a new song he was working on, "Back in the Saddle Again." Which was what Autry was once his legal problems with Hollywood were resolved.

The Palace Theater, opened in 1921, remained in business until 1993, forty years after Autry made his last movie.

The singer had turned to the newer medium of television in the early 1950s, eventually retiring to run his many business interests. For a guy once forced to play a small town for $100, Autry went on to do pretty well for himself. In 1995, three years before his death, his assets were reported at $320 million. Not bad for a tumbling tumbleweed from East Texas.

Laughing Matters

Brownfield's Roosevelt Riot

An article with a Fort Worth dateline published in a Sunday edition of the *New York Herald* caught the eye of President Theodore Roosevelt as he sat in his home at Oyster Bay, New York in the summer of 1908.

The four-paragraph dispatch, which dealt with an incident reported as having occurred in the then five-year-old South Plains town of Brownfield, struck the president as bully news, something he wanted to share with his friend Senator Henry Cabot Lodge. The following Tuesday, noting his "immense delight" with the piece, Roosevelt included the full text of the article in a letter to the senator:

> *Fort Worth, Texas, Saturday* [August 15, 1908]. *Word reached here today from Brownfield, in Terry County, western Texas, that residents there on Thursday erected a life-sized statute of President Roosevelt after a street fight in which 50 shots were fired. One person was killed and nine others were wounded. The statue represents Mr. Roosevelt in hunting costume and stands on the town square.*

After noting that Brownfield lay one hundred miles from the nearest railroad and had a population of 1,500, who were mostly ranchers, cowboys or farmers, the article explained the issue behind the battle over the statue:

> *The erection of the statue was vigorously opposed by Democrats and some Republicans, but it had already been ordered from Denver by a citizen's*

President Theodore Roosevelt got a big kick out of the Brownfield "riot" story. *Library of Congress.*

committee which refused to turn from its plans. The unveiling was opposed because...Roosevelt was still President and because the Democrats wanted a [William Jennings] *Bryan statue on the opposite side of the square and the town could not afford both statues.*

The *Herald* story went on to report that the anti–Roosevelt statue crowd had at first stolen the statue and buried it. But the pro-Roosevelt folks had recovered the piece, cleaned it up and placed it on the courthouse square.

During the dedication ceremonies, "a band of cowboys made a rush and met a determined crowd. Revolvers, fists and clubs were freely used but the statue was not disturbed."

Finally, after ten people had been shot, cooler heads prevailed. At a mass meeting following the riot, "a compromise was effected whereby it was agreed that should Bryan be elected, his statue should be placed near that of Roosevelt."

Concluding his letter to the honorable senator from New York, Roosevelt said he had never heard of the statue before reading the story about it in the *Herald*. Indeed, he added, he had never even heard of Brownfield.

But measuring up to his tough guy, living-life-to-the-hilt image, the president said, "I think there is something delightful beyond words in the idea of this sudden erection of a statue of me in hunting costume, at the cost of a riot in which one man was killed and nine wounded, and the final compromise by which it was agreed upon to put up another statue of Bryan in case he was elected."

Writing that he wondered what the statue looked like, Roosevelt concluded: "Who, with a sense of humor and a real zest for life [clearly describing himself], would not be glad to be prominent in American politics at the outset of the Twentieth Century?"

Nearly two decades later, writer R.J. Pendleton decided to visit Brownfield to see the statue that had caused a riot and claimed a life. His camera ready, Pendleton drove around the square looking for a bronze Teddy Roosevelt. But, as he wrote, "no masterpiece of the sculptor's art was anywhere to be seen." Thinking the statue might have been moved, Pendleton drove the town's other major streets. Still, no Teddy.

Beginning to think that Bryan's supporters might have prevailed and succeeded in stealing or destroying the monument, Pendleton went to the office of the *Brownfield News* to see if the local editor knew what had become of the trouble-causing statue.

When Pendleton asked about the statue, the editor broke into a smile bigger than Roosevelt's favorite grin.

"There's nothing to it," the editor said. "Some reporter with a vivid imagination must have made up the yarn and then looked around for a good place in which to locate it and picked Brownfield."

The editor told Pendleton that Senator Lodge had never really bought into the statue story, though the nation's twenty-sixth president apparently believed every word of it. As Pendleton concluded, whoever dreamed up the tale must have had "too much regard for the truth to drag it out on every paltry occasion."

Lamesa:
Home of the Chicken-Fried Steak...Not!

Ever wonder how a legend gets started?

I had a small role in the creation of what has become one of Texas's most enduring pieces of "fakelore"—the story of the invention of the chicken-fried steak.

Larry BeSaw with a framed copy of the chicken-fried steak story he just plain made up. *Photo courtesy Lauren Levi.*

It all began back in the 1970s with a friendly argument between me and my still good friend Larry BeSaw. Larry grew up in Cooke County, where for a long time his parents operated a classic mom and pop café.

Eschewing the food service industry, Larry had sense enough to pursue a career in journalism, which is how we met. Both of us drew weekly paychecks as staff writers for the *Austin American-Statesman*.

Larry's childhood exposure to classic Texas fare helped him develop a lifetime appreciation of good groceries, particularly chicken-friend steaks. And that's where Larry and I did not see ribeye to ribeye.

While my grandparents fried steaks (which people of their generation tended to call "chops"), I grew up with an appreciation of a well-smoked but medium-rare grilled steak. Why have a lesser cut of meat dolled up with flour and then cooked in grease if you could enjoy a juicy piece of red meat as God intended it, warmed just enough so that it no longer mooed?

Over countless cans of adult beverages, Larry and I debated the relative merits of a rare steak versus a chicken-fried steak. Neither of us could sway the other.

We worked for a daily newspaper, but during the holidays, with the exception of the occasional calamity, the flow of news usually slows considerably as people take off to be with their families. Knowing an easy way to fill space when she saw it, in early January 1976, Jane Ulrich, the newspaper's lifestyle editor, commissioned Larry to write a story on chicken-fried steak.

Back then, CBS's *60 Minutes* had a weekly feature called "Point/Counterpoint" in which two people with strong but opposing views not so politely expressed their opinions to viewers. When I heard that Larry would be writing that story, I proposed writing a "Counter Point" view on our ongoing culinary differences.

Happy at the prospect of filling even more space, Jane readily assented. Hearing of our project, colleague Arnold Garcia offered to weigh in with his argument that menudo trumped either one of our meat preferences. Realizing she had now managed to fill the entire front page of her section, Jane said that would be fine and dandy.

Garcia and I wrote essays that deservedly have been forgotten (well, I was sort of proud of my assertion that the *Titanic* crew member tasked with keeping an eye out for icebergs had just eaten a chicken-fried steak before beginning what would be his final watch), but Larry went on to produce what has proven a timeless classic.

In support of his thesis that chicken-fried steak is superior to any other method of beef preparation, Larry created from whole cloth a 100 percent bogus history of the chicken-fried steak. As he reported, the dish was invented by one Jimmy Don Perkins, an unemployed drawbridge oiler working as a short-order cook in the South Plains town of Lamesa.

The momentous event, the Big Bang of the Texas greasy food chain, occurred in 1911 at a local café called Ethel's Home Cooking. Larry offered that the eatery got its name because whenever anyone asked about Ethel, the proprietor answered that she was home cooking.

Not that Jimmy Don was all that smart. He merely proved yet again the importance of the lowly comma by misinterpreting the waitress's hastily scribbled order reading "chicken, fried steak" and chicken fried a steak.

Ben Sargent, who went on to win a Pulitzer Prize for his political cartoons, drew the illustrations that accompanied the piece, which appeared on January 11, 1976. Judging by word-of-mouth feedback, our editors and the newspaper's readers liked the story. That was that, we all assumed.

At the time, the *American-Statesman* and many other Texas newspapers carried a syndicated weekly Texas history column by the late Jack Maguire called "Talk of Texas." Imagine our surprise when two or three weeks following the appearance of our story package, Maguire told his many readers the story behind the creation of the chicken-friend steak. Of course, he forgot to say where he stole it from. And he apparently didn't get that it was just a joke.

After that, the tale spread faster than spilled cream gravy. Former *American-Statesman* humor columnist Mike Kelley was the first to point out in print that the story of the birth of the chicken-friend steak was complete fiction, but that has not stopped the falling dominos of literary larceny.

Larry has a growing collection of articles telling the Lamesa tale as truth. The Dawson County Museum in Lamesa has a framed copy of our chicken-fried steak story on display, and there has been talk of having Larry come to Lamesa to judge a chicken-fried-steak cooking contest. Some of the buyers of the bogus story include the online encyclopedia Wikipedia, the august *Washington Post* and the stately Smithsonian Institution, which in an exhibit on Texas foods at least used the word "purportedly" in recounting Larry's story.

"Of all the stories I've written over the years," Larry says, "I hate to think the one piece of writing I'll be remembered for is a lie. I just wish I got royalties, or even credit, every time some other writer steals that story."

One Famous Son of Fritch

Starting in the mid-1930s and continuing well into the '50s, Fritch must have had some of the most mannerly, patient postal patrons in the country.

Not that folks in this Panhandle town between Amarillo and Borger didn't occasionally get annoyed by slow mail delivery, a damaged parcel or misdirected letters, but customers must have been very careful about expressing any displeasure when Mrs. Cleo Lee worked as postmistress.

Folks said she'd been a vaudeville performer in her salad days. Petite, good looking and well dressed, she sang, played a piano and chain-smoked Camels. At the height of her career, she'd first come to the Panhandle in a fancy new flivver on tour with her act. When she later returned during the Depression, the story goes, she and a new husband arrived dead broke. She had lost her looks and gained weight. And not all of her baggage was the kind a person could pack in a suitcase. In other words, she'd had a hard life.

The woman who took charge of Fritch's post office in 1934 may have had something of a mysterious past, but one thing about her was an open book: her attitude.

Having switched from cigarettes to Headliner cigars, Mrs. Lee had a reputation for "going postal" long before that term entered the vernacular.

She never went berserk and gunned down her customers, but she could cuss the proverbial blue streak when something happened that she didn't like. Unruly children particularly got her goat.

Like many Texas towns, Fritch owed its existence to the railroad. In 1926, the Rock Island Railroad began working on a spur line between Amarillo and Liberal, Kansas. By July 1, 1927, the tracks had reached a point thirty-six miles northeast of Amarillo near the Moore-Hutchinson County line. The company named the depot in honor of H.C. (Fred) Fritch, a Rock Island big wheel.

Workers kept laying track beyond Fritch, and by October 1, 1929, the new route across the Panhandle had been completed. Though the stock market crashed later that month, the railroad wanted to develop a town site adjacent to its depot and bought land for that purpose. Survey stakes marking streets and lots went down in 1933.

Fritch's promoter was H.P. Newport, a major player in the earlier development of Ponca City, Oklahoma. Newport also served as Fritch's first postmaster. But selling real estate appealed to Newport more than selling stamps. Several others held the position briefly before Joe Lee, Newport's son-in-law, got the appointment. Lee and his wife, Cleo, had recently arrived from Kansas.

Oil had been discovered in Hutchinson County in 1926, and the new town of Borger, thirteen miles from Frith, had sprung up as fast as tarpaper could be nailed on wood. While Borger got most of the benefit of the oil boom, Fritch lay closer to the natural gas drilling camps.

The Texoma Natural Gas Co., headquartered in Chicago, sent its payroll in cash to Fritch every two weeks. One week, Postmaster Lee made a special delivery of the gas company's payroll to himself and departed Fritch for elsewhere. Arrested the next day in Amarillo, he ended up going back to Kansas, this time to the federal prison at Fort Leavenworth.

Cleo, who had no complicity in her husband's mail theft, was appointed postmistress to replace him. The fact that her uncle was U.S. postmaster general may have had something to do with her getting the job.

While Mrs. Lee could be crankier than a tool pusher with a hangover headache, people who entered the post office when she was in the back sorting mail often heard her singing in a beautiful voice seemingly unaffected by her heavy smoking. The melody mingled with cigar smoke inside the corrugated metal post office.

Unlike her husband and other predecessors on the job, Mrs. Lee ran the Fritch post office for twenty-one years, from 1934 to her death in 1955.

She left behind twenty cats and four or five dogs, supposedly stipulating in her will that all her animals be shot after her death. Whether that actually happened is not known, but it adds detail to the portrait of her character.

In 1959, with construction soon to begin on Sanford Dam, the structure across the Canadian River that created Lake Meredith, Fritch incorporated as a general law city with a mayor-council government. And it got a larger post office to handle the growth spurt that came with the new federally operated recreational area.

Not many people are still around who remember Fritch's colorful former postmaster, but a lot of people have laughed at the stories told by the most famous son of Fritch—comedian Ron White of Blue Collar Comedy Tour fame. Born in Fritch in 1956, White sometimes riffs on his youthful experiences in the Panhandle.

He's probably never heard of Mrs. Lee, but he sure has one thing in common with her: an appreciation of a good cigar.

High Plains Ingenuity

Bone Roads

Building a highway in 1879 was a little easier than it is these days.

A twenty-first-century roadway involves engineering, public hearings, right of way acquisition, environmental surveys, archaeological work, innovative financing and, finally, construction.

In 1935, as Texas readied for the celebration of its centennial of independence from Mexico, the son of the man who laid out the first road across the South Plains told the story. Bog Smith recalled how his father, H.C. "Hank" Smith, along with Charlie Howse, got public transportation off to its start on the Llano Estacado.

On the plains, the difficulty faced was not a lack of suitable terrain for travel but rather the very vastness of the land. Miles of waving grass on flat land were no less intractable than the open sea. A person could easily get lost, and many did. In times of extreme weather, this could prove fatal and occasionally did.

When a hardy group of Quakers settled a community in Crosby County they called Estacado, Smith decided to lay off a road from his residence to the new town.

After Smith recruited Howse as his helper, the two men left the Smith place one morning in an ox-drawn wagon. They stopped periodically to fill the wagon with bleached buffalo bones, the legacy of the soon-to-be-completed slaughter of the bison. When they had a wagonful, they stopped and piled all the bones to make a road marker that could be seen for miles in either direction in good weather.

Then they traveled on, gathering more bones. Stopping after a mile, they made another big bone heap. The two men continued the process until they reached Estacado and the South Plains had its first-known marked roadway.

How long the buffalo bone mile markers lasted is not known, but most of the buffalo remnants on the plains vanished in the next wave of land exploitation—the collection of bones for shipment east to be ground into fertilizer. Those who made their living doing this were called bone pickers, and it was not a particularly complimentary title.

Estacado did not last a whole lot longer than the buffalo bones that assisted travelers in finding it. It at least had the distinction of being the first town on the South Plains (Mobeetie and Tascosa were both on the North Plains, though that term has fallen out of usage). In 1886, when Crosby County was organized, it became the county seat. But that status held only until 1891, when Emma became the new county capital. Emma, too, faded, and Crosbyton is now the county seat.

COW PATTIES

When meteorologists start forecasting the first real fall weather, sellers of corded firewood appear on the roadsides to cash in on city-dwelling homeowners either without hardwood trees to cut or chainsaws with which to cut them.

Someone has always made a little money selling firewood in Texas. If you are handy with a saw and have a lot of trees on your property, harvesting oak on a commercial basis makes perfect sense. And with increasing urbanization, the enterprise has grown in popularity.

For much of Texas's history, though, getting firewood posed no particular problem—at least across the right half of the state looking north. Campers could find plenty of wood along creek and riverbanks or under the oak motts that dotted the prairie before juniper and mesquite proliferated.

On the High Plains, with trees scarcer than sinners at a revival, finding fire fuel took more effort. While folks traveling in a wagon might haul an emergency supply of split wood, travelers, scouts and cowboys soon realized that a ready source of fuel surrounded them: buffalo chips.

Before commercial hunters killed them off, hundreds of thousands of buffalo grazed the native grasses covering the seemingly endless Panhandle landscape. After getting the nutrition their huge bodies needed from the grass they ate, the bison disposed of the end product in plentitude.

In time, buffalo dung dissolved into the soil, keeping the ground fertile for the next growing season. But before that happened, the product hardened in the sun, becoming something that could be easily picked up. Early on, Indians figured out that this natural fertilizer made good fuel. Buffalo hunters quickly adopted the technique.

"Sometime before sunset we began to look for a place suitable to camp," former buffalo hunter George Andrew Gordon later recalled. "The place being selected, and the horses picketed, the young men set to work to collect fuel. If wood was not convenient, buffalo chips were generally plentiful."

When cattle replaced buffalo on the plains, cow chips in turn replaced buffalo chips as a ready source of British thermal units. Of course, cowboys didn't know BTUs from balky mules, but they knew what it was like to be hungry or cold without a fire.

Fortunately, a thousand-pound cow can produce from sixty to ninety pounds of manure a day. Once the moisture content drops below 20 percent, it makes fine fuel. Just don't expect the same sort of pleasing aroma that comes from an oak or mesquite fire.

Well into his old age, Harold B. Campbell wrote about cow chip cooking in a family history called *Spotted Stripes* he self-published in 1992.

"There is a considerable difference in the quality of cow chips," Campbell wrote. "During the spring when the grass was watery and green the chips were splattery and no good. They were called spring dimples."

Cow chips improved in the summer but still ran pretty thin. Panhandle settlers called those "summer flats."

Ah, but come fall and winter, the time of greatest need, cow patties reached their prime. The grass remnants they contained had cured, and the moisture level was low. "Tall, thick and solid," Campbell wrote, "these were called fall browns."

Everyone in his family chipped in, so to speak, in collecting fall browns. The family headed to the prairie in a wagon with sideboards, and "all who was big enough helped load the wagons."

Though usually in ample supply, getting cow patties to burn could be tricky on windy days.

Dick and Ada Tisdale bought four sections of land in Hartley County near Channing in 1901. One day, Ada gathered chips preparatory to cooking lunch for her husband, who was out working cattle. No novice at building campfires in Central Texas where she grew up, she lit the fire, but the wind blew it out. She lit it again, and the same thing happened.

When Dick arrived for his midday meal, he found his wife crying. Wiping away her tears, he dug a trench and kicked in the cow chips. Soon they had a nice fire followed by a hot lunch.

Families depending on cow patties for energy learned to look for sweet spots where the pickings were good. Recalling the hard days of the Great Depression, Homer C. Beck wrote an item for a book on the history of Sherman County about how his family depended on a windmill for cowchips. The mill, at the base of a bluff that offered shelter from the cold north wind, attracted a lot of cattle both for the water the mill pumped and the protein-rich cottonseed cake the landowner used to supplement the hay he put out.

"We children spent Saturdays all through the winter down by that mill gathering chips," Beck recalled. "We used old washtubs with a three-foot rope tied to the handle, and we would drag it around looking for chips."

Once each child had a full tub, they dumped the chips in the back of their father's 1925 Chevrolet truck and went back for another load until they had the truck full.

"We used the chips sparingly in the winter by going to bed soon after dark and not trying to keep the house warm enough for reading or visiting," he wrote.

Demand for chips decreased in the summer, when the kids only had to collect enough for their mother's kitchen stove.

If a steak grilled over cow patties doesn't sound appetizing, beneath dried pasture plops is a good place to look for fishing worms. Obviously, cow patties make good fertilizer. Also, cow patties sprayed with gold paint make inexpensive gifts for people who seem to have everything.

Additionally, cow chip tossing is considered a sporting event in some circles. All you need is spray paint to mark some circles on the ground (or use a hula hoop) and a supply of dried cow patties. Establish a starting line twenty or so feet from the target, and let the fun begin. The winner is the person who can chunk a chip and land it in or near the target. Each contestant gets three tries.

Low Tech v. High Tech in the 1890s

As anyone who has ever puzzled over what to do next when his computer screen fairly screams to him that he has committed a "Fatal Error" knows, technology can cause anxiety.

High Plains Ingenuity

Learning to cope with progress has been a problem since the beginning of the industrial age, though it probably has grown more acute with each new invention.

Bena Jones had a brief, if unsettling, run-in with high tech in the early 1890s.

Born in Pittsburg in 1866, she had come as a child to Topeka, Kansas, with her family. In 1885, she was married to Joseph Jones. A native of Wales, Jones had immigrated with his family to the United States when he was eight. They, too, settled in Kansas, but in 1880, Jones left home for Mobeetie on the eastern edge of the Texas Panhandle.

Five years later, back in Topeka, Jones married Bena. The couple returned to Texas by stagecoach from Dodge City.

They stayed in Mobeetie, but in 1890, Jones bought a ranch in Hansford County. After their first child was born in 1892, they moved to the ranch six miles south of what is now Gruver.

By then, the Indians and the buffalo were gone, but the Panhandle remained only sparsely settled. For the Jones family, food and supplies lay a long wagon ride away in the community of Hansford.

On one of those trips from their ranch to town, Bena Jones encountered something she had not seen before: a telephone line. The line, actually two wires, ran along a fence line. At each gate, the wires were strung overhead between tall posts.

The road leading to town went through one of those gates. Leaving her children in the buggy, Mrs. Jones walked cautiously to the gate, opened it real fast and hastened back to the wagon.

Snapping the reins, she shot the buggy through the gate like a horizontal bolt of lightning.

Pulling her horse to a halt about two hundred feet beyond the gate, she reversed the process, carefully and quickly closing the gate as her children waited safely in the distance.

Her fear was that the telephone lines radiated a dangerous electrical charge that might be harmful to anyone having prolonged exposure to it. However, when she got to the store in Old Hansford, the proprietor assured her that she faced no danger from the new method of communication.

Telephone lines were not dangerous, but a raging blizzard was. The first winter on their new ranch was so cold that the young couple had to stack their furniture on one side of their ranch house and move their horses into the other side. Otherwise, the animals would have frozen to death.

One day, as the Jones children played outside during a more temperate time of year, they heard horses and tinkling bells. Peeping over the stone wall of their corral, the children saw Indians riding down the hill toward their ranch house.

Though a hostile Indian had not been in the area for more than a decade and a half, Texans had not forgotten their nearly sixty-year struggle with the Comanches and other warlike tribes.

The children ran to report the "attack," but their father took the news calmly. He knew the reservation Indians from Oklahoma meant no harm and let them camp on his land for several days. In turn, the Indians invited the Jones family to join them for a meal.

When the children outgrew the small country school near their ranch, Jones moved his family to Guymon. But he continued to run the ranch in Hansford County until his death at age fifty-seven in 1919. His widow kept the ranch running for another forty years. She died on January 4, 1951.

TRAVEL TRAILERS PANHANDLE STYLE

They didn't come with air conditioning, toilets, showers, generators, satellite TV or microwaves, but many an early day Panhandle farm family lived temporarily in mule-drawn wooden trailers.

These four-wheelers had to do with making a living, not affordable housing or the pursuit of recreation. Early in the twentieth century, farmers on the High Plains began converting vast acreages of what had been ranch land into wheat-growing operations. By summer, the golden grain stood ready for harvesting.

Bringing in acre after acre of grain amounted to a huge undertaking. The state-of-the-art eventually improved beyond scythes swung by hand to horse-drawn reapers and mechanical threshers. Next came steam-powered machinery and finally equipment driven by gasoline motors.

It not being economically feasible for every farmer to own equipment used only once a year, capitalism filled the void, and the business of professional harvesting came into being. Teams and equipment moved from farm to farm during the season, harvesting for hire.

A committee-published history of Carlton, a semi-ghost town farther downstate in Hamilton County, described the process:

> *Most farmers had already cut, bundled and shocked their grain which now stood in row and after row across broad fields. Wagons with their special grain-racks moved about the shocks being loaded into great, towering ricks*

by men with hay forks who "pitched up" to the wagon drivers. Each loaded wagon proceeding in turn to the huge threshing machine which upon being fed a steady stream of bundles, rattled, shook, whirred and chopped as if devouring each grain-laden sheaf.

Even with such machinery, the effort required a considerable amount of manpower. Itinerant threshing crew members traveled from county to county across the Panhandle and South Plains and "toiled, sweated and joked and laughed throughout the long hot days."

The crews had to break for meals, of course.

As one family historian wrote for her clan's website, "Additional to the machinery, there was a cook shack, which was a shack on wheels."

In 1956, Rosa Lowry told Canyon writer Pollyanna B. Hughes about the trailer her husband, Bud, acquired for use during the harvest.

"Bud heard of a cook shack that he might buy," Lowery recalled. "He paid $45 for it, and that was a lot of money for that time and place. But I was so very happy when he went to get it."

Fourteen feet long and half as wide, the wooden shack with a rounded roof sat on a wagon bed pulled by two mules. It had a door on one end and a sliding window on the other end for food service. Lowry installed a fold-

Grain elevators remain a Panhandle fixture, but not the early day trailers for wheat harvesters. *Author's collection.*

down table on the side of the shack and used a canvas wagon sheet to make a covered porch.

The trailer slept seven. Mrs. Lowery placed a bed on one side that her three daughters shared. The couple's oldest boy slept on a pallet on the floor of the trailer, and Bud and Rosa slept with their infant son on a cot on the other side of the wagon. The hired hands spent their nights under the stars on bedrolls.

Henry O. Howe, who as a young man homesteaded land near Guymon in the Oklahoma Panhandle, had fond memories of cook shack trailers. When harvest time came around, he went to Texas and worked on a threshing crew for an Ochiltree County farmer.

The boss's daughter ran the rolling cook shack. Howe made enough money at threshing to come back to the same farm the following year. Not only did he earn a good wage, he also developed a fondness for both the grub and the pretty cook. Following that second season, Howe decided he could find other ways to earn a living but married the cook. They went on to have fourteen children and stayed married for many years, separated only by death.

When more affordable motor-driven combines (so named because they handled both reaping and separation of grain) came on the market, the traveling threshing business became a thing of the past.

But the notion of a shack on wheels endured, only now they're called mobile homes or RVs.

When Coins Fell from the Sky

Once upon a time, a shower of shiny gold coins fell from the sky over Palo Duro Canyon State Park south of Amarillo.

No, really. This isn't a fairy tale. That actually happened one Saturday in the late spring of 1949, a decade and a half after the scenic and history-rich Panhandle park opened to the public on July 4, 1934. Of course, the coins that rained down on the canyon that day were only brass with gold-looking plating called "goldine."

Even so, the metallic manna-from-heaven-style event drew a big crowd to the rim of the canyon and may have netted two lucky people all-expense-paid, eight-day vacations to Havana, Cuba. That was back during the long dictatorship of President Fulgencio Batista, when Havana was a wide-open party town controlled by the American mafia.

A visitor surveys Palo Duro from the rim of the canyon. *Author's collection.*

On May 28, 1949, an airplane flew over the nation's second-largest canyon and dropped ten thousand coins over the park, which then covered some sixteen thousand acres and now includes nearly thirty thousand acres. A thousand of the coins would be redeemable for prizes collectively valued at $10,000.

Once the coins had been dropped, Governor Beauford H. Jester cut a ribbon at the entrance to the park to trigger a twentieth-century "gold" rush and the earliest large-scale effort to position the canyon as a major Panhandle tourist destination.

Park officials were bracing for a turnout of 100,000 people that day, but whether that large a crowd actually showed up was not reported. No matter the number, the driver of each car entering the park had to pay forty-two cents, plus twenty-four cents for any additional adult in the vehicle. Children got in for twelve cents.

As soon as the visitors could drive down to the floor of the canyon and get their cars parked, the treasure hunt began. What they hoped to find was a coin that on one side bore the legend "Texas Palo Duro Canyon Treasure Hunt 1949." The other side featured a raised image of the park's most famous landmark, the towering rock formation called the Lighthouse. A number had been stamped across the lower part of the Lighthouse near the bottom of the coin. All the coins with numbers ending in seven netted the finder a prize if claimed by Labor Day 1949.

The Lighthouse, Palo Duro's iconic landmark. *Author's collection.*

Other than the grand prizes, finders had a shot at season passes to Amarillo Gold Sox home games, a $250 diamond ring donated by an Amarillo jeweler and two registered quarter horses from Panhandle rancher Glenn L. Casey.

An organization called the Palo Duro Canyon Boosters Club sponsored the effort. Contemporary newspaper coverage in advance of and after the event doesn't reveal whose brainchild this campaign had been, but whoever dreamed it up hit a public relations home run. It might have been F.W. "Fist" Ansley (1899–1979), chairman of the club.

Since Braniff Airways had put up the top prizes, the pioneer aviation company doubtless played a role in the publicity campaign. In fact, some PR type at the company's Dallas headquarters may well have come up with the idea of cashing in on the fact that 1949 marked the centennial of the great California gold rush.

"The Palo Duro 'gold rush' is being held by the boosters club to solicit membership and appropriate funds and gifts to advertise Palo Duro Canyon attractions throughout the country," read a news release widely published in Texas newspapers before the event. "A program of events will be scheduled to attract people to this region and to draw steady tourist trade to the Panhandle."

The organization hoped to gain as many new members as the number of coins dropped from above, each membership costing one dollar. Whether that happened was not reported, but given that people are generally more interested in getting something for nothing than spending a dollar when that much money could buy nearly a quarter tank of gasoline, it's hard to believe the boosters reached their hoped-for number.

Six decades later, park visitors still occasionally find one of the coins from the Palo Duro Gold Rush of 1949. Unfortunately, though nice collectibles, they are no longer redeemable for prizes.

Getting There and Back

Lonnie Houston's Last Ride

When fourteen-year-old Lonnie Houston left Mobeetie with his mail sacks that September day, the trail south to Clarendon cut through a veritable ocean of grass. The Indians and the buffalo they had survived on had been gone from the Panhandle for more than a decade, but the unbroken landscape seemingly stretched on endlessly.

Three weeks earlier, in late August 1888, the area around Clarendon had enjoyed what one newspaper correspondent called "a splendid rain." The moisture from above, the writer continued, had resulted in "luxuriant grasses, to the great joy of the cattleman."

The main thing on Lonnie's mind, however, would have been getting to Clarendon and back with the weekly mail. Making a 130-mile round trip through open, mostly uninhabited country was dangerous work, but Lonnie's family needed the money.

Lonnie was the oldest of four motherless children. His father's work kept him away from home much of the time, which left Lonnie as the man of the house. But like his father, Lonnie also had a job. It's not known what his father did, but Lonnie worked as a mail carrier on the Wheeler County–Clarendon route, which had only had a post office since that January.

On September 13, Lonnie hitched his horse to the buggy he used to haul the mail and set out for Clarendon, some sixty-five miles to the south. A good horse could trot up to ten miles an hour on level ground, but most horses didn't have more than twenty-five miles a day in them. Lonnie should have spent the night at or near an old stage station near LeFors, which lay

This was how the Panhandle looked to Lonnie Houston when he carried the mail from Mobeetie to Clarendon. *Author's collection.*

about halfway between Mobeetie and his destination in Donley County, but he apparently pressed on, possibly walking his horse more slowly. Maybe he intended to camp for the night somewhere along the way.

Whatever his plans, as he rolled along through the waving grass, Lonnie began to realize that something was wrong with his horse. The animal's gait steadily slowed, and he began whinnying and pitching his head.

"Seeing that he could not travel any further," the *Hutchinson* [Kansas] *Daily News* later reported, "the boy took [the horse] out of the harness and made him as comfortable as he could. Then, true to his trust, he took the mail sacks on his own slender shoulders and walked the remaining distance— thirteen miles—and delivered the mail in safety to the postmaster."

In Clarendon, Lonnie borrowed a young, only partially broken pony from a friend and rode back to where he had left his horse and buggy. Reaching the spot, he found that his horse had died.

"He then hitched up the pony, thinking he would be as easily managed in harness as under the saddle," the newspaper continued, "but, never having been driven, the pony at once began to plunge and kick, upsetting the vehicle."

Lonnie fell hard on the ground as the horse continued in its mindless frenzy. Before he could get up, the panicking animal kicked the teenager on his forehead, killing him.

Horse- or mule-drawn wagons like these hauled mail across the Panhandle. *Author's collection.*

The newspaper did not say how long the youngster lay there next to the wrecked buggy and bucking horse, but at some point a passerby found Lonnie's body. Readily discerning he could do nothing for the boy, the man hurried on to town to notify authorities.

Reaching Clarendon, the man reported his discovery to someone identified only as Mr. Henry, who in turn notified H.B. White.

"All that tender hands could do was done for the little mangled body," the newspaper said, "which was brought into Clarendon last night [September 14.]"

The newspaper story did not say whether Lonnie had lived in Mobeetie or Clarendon. Neither did it report where the youngster was buried. A search of online cemetery records for both Donley and Wheeler County revealed no grave for a Lonnie Houston, though the Old Mobeetie Cemetery does have the grave of a Louise Houston, who died at the age of two in 1887. She could have been Lonnie's little sister.

While little is known about the Panhandle teenager who died carrying the mail, information regarding rural mail service and child labor is easier to find. Lonnie had worked for an independent contractor who had secured from the U.S. Post Office Department the exclusive right to transport mail along a fixed route, a task the government stipulated had to be handled with "celerity, certainty and security." In the age of handwritten government documents, bureaucrats quickly tired of writing all three words into each mail contract and started using asteriks instead. Soon they became known as Star Routes.

While recognition of the need to either protect children in the workplace or keep them out of it altogether dates to the early 1880s, it did not become illegal to hire children until passage of a federal law in 1916 that prevented interstate commerce of items manufactured by anyone younger than fourteen. But two years later, the U.S. Supreme Court ruled the law unconstitutional, and another twenty years went by until hiring young children finally went on the books. That was in 1938, when President Franklin D. Roosevelt signed the Fair Labor Standards Act into law. That measure sets the minimum employable age at fourteen.

It was later claimed that one James Cornelius Short had been the first man to carry the mail from Mobeetie to Lefors, but he didn't come to the Panhanlde until 1889, the year after Lonnie Houston died trying to do his job. In Short's time, he made the run once a week, either by horse or buggy. Unlike the teenager who preceeded him, he lived to tell about his experiences, but he had definitely earned his pay. Sometimes he made the long trip in pouring rain or blowing snow with only a single postcard in his mailbag.

The Amarillo "Symphony"

Santa Fe Train Number One, with a 3751-class 4-8-4 steam engine up front, pulled up to the red-roofed, Mission revival–style Amarillo station on time.

One of the people stepping off the train at the busy depot was William Gibson, a Santa Fe employee traveling on a company pass. With his small suitcase in one hand and his well-worn tool and instrument valise in the other, Gibson walked from the station to the nearby Capitol Hotel at Fourth and Pierce. The Herring, across the street, rose higher and had three times as many rooms, but Gibson liked the two-hundred-room Capitol. At the front desk, Gibson went through a familiar routine: he asked for a south-side room on the fourth floor or higher.

As soon as he closed the door behind him, Gibson walked to the window and looked out. His room, as he knew it would, looked down on the busy Santa Fe yard. The roundhouse had thirty-two train stalls and was almost always full. In the distance, Gibson saw a plume of black smoke as a freight train hit an eastbound grade on a big curve. After taking in the view for a

Downtown Amarillo in the 1940s, when the Panhandle's largest city was still a passenger train hub. *Author's collection.*

moment, he raised the window a few inches. It opened easily—wood did not often swell with moisture on the High Plains. At nearly 3,700 feet above sea level, spring and summer nights are usually cool and humidity-free.

On this night, the wind blew strong from the southeast, sucking through the cracked window. Gibson liked the fresh night air, but he had opened the window more to let in sound.

Number One had boarded passengers in Amarillo and was moving slowly through the Amarillo yard. Gibson checked his watch. It was still on time. Its

Santa Fe Railroad trains rumbled through Amarillo and other Panhandle cities around the clock. *Author's collection.*

hogger—railroad talk for engineer—blasted the whistle as the train headed toward the Twenty-fourth Street crossing.

One long, two shorts and then a continuous blast until the engine cleared the crossing. The shrill sound created by the high-pressure steam echoed off the concrete grain elevators lining the tracks and the high-rise office buildings along busy Polk Street. The whistle was music to the railroad man's ears. With tongue in cheek, he called it the "Amarillo Symphony."

Periodically through the night, other trains moved in and out of Amarillo as most of the city slept. In addition to the Santa Fe track, main lines of the Fort Worth and Denver and the Rock Island Line intersected at Amarillo. The piercing notes of train whistles spread across the city and cut onto the vastness of the plains.

For several generations of Amarilloans, the whistle signals of the steam engine either comforted them at night like a homemade quilt or haunted their dreams. For some, the whistles made good company, dispelling any sense of isolation; others heard the trains and felt lonesome, remembering or imagining trips taken or not taken. For all Amarilloans, those whistles—long since replaced by more prosaic air horns—represent the sound of a city's history.

Amarillo is the largest city in Texas owing its existence solely to the railroad. Houston, Dallas, San Antonio, El Paso, Fort Worth and Austin all had other reasons to be, though railroads certainly benefited each. But Amarillo would not exist—or if it did, it probably would not have amounted to much—had it not been for the iron road.

Amarillo's First Airmail

William H. Bush—industrialist and Panhandle ranch owner—heard someone knocking on the door of his Chicago residence at eleven thirty that night. Peering outside, he was relieved to see a gray-uniformed postman and went to open the door.

"Special delivery," the mail carrier announced, handing him an envelope with a red-and-blue border.

The letter was from his brother, James, in Amarillo. Opening it, William saw it had been written the day before, October 24, 1930.

"Dear Brother," it began, "I am mailing you this letter by air mail. This is the first trip that the air mail makes direct from Amarillo. I am sending it special delivery and they tell me you should get it Saturday night or Sunday morning."

Downtown Amarillo about the time it first got airmail service in 1930. *Author's collection.*

Indeed, it was Saturday night, October 25. With five cents in postage to cover the plane trip and an additional twenty cents for special delivery, the envelope had left the Panhandle shortly before 8:00 a.m. that day. The plane carrying it and other north- and east-bound airmail landed in Kansas City, where postal workers transferred the bag containing the letter to Bush to another plane. That aircraft reached the Windy City at 9:30 p.m. From the airport, the letter and others went by truck to the North Side post office. When it arrived there, a carrier drove it to Bush's residence for delivery only fifteen hours and thirty minutes after it left Amarillo.

While that is snail-like compared to e-mail, it was incredibly fast for 1930, especially to the Bush brothers.

"When you first came to Texas," James reminded William, "you could only come part way by train and had to use the stage coach which today is obsolete. Not only the airplane of today but also the automobile had not been thought of."

Even when Amarillo first got rail service, it was not unusual for a train to be as much as a day late, he said.

"When you came here first there was no Amarilo," James continnued, "and when I came here in 1903 it was only 1,500 [in population]. There was not a paved street, a white-way light or a cement sidewalk in the place, or a fenced highway that extended over two miles from town."

While the letter James mailed to William was in the first bag sent directly from Amarillo via airmail, the Panhandle city had received its first airmail via a Transcontinental and Western Air Ford tri-motor passenger plane that arrived in May 1929.

Regular airmail service began the following year, on October 25, with the plane that carried Bush's letter to Chicago. In anticipation of the big event, Amarillo and Panhandle residents had been dropping off airmail letters at the post office for a week so they could receive the first-day-of-service cancellation.

"Mail will travel from Amarillo to New York in 22 hours, against 52 hours for rail time," the *Amarillo Daily News* reported on October 23. "It will go to Chicago in nine hours and 40 minutes, and to Los Angeles in nine hours."

Two days later, at 7:57 a.m., postmaster W.C. Kenyon hefted the first pouch of airmail onto the first flight out of Amarillo's English Field. "Before night it will be scattered across the mid-west to Columbus, Ohio, there to go to the Atlantic coast," the article continued.

At the Air Mail Day ceremony celebrating the inaugural flights, U.S. congressman Marvin Jones predicted that Amarillo would become an aviation center.

"It will become known as the crossroads of the air," Jones said.

The newspaper said that six mail planes would be stopping in Amarillo every day. Regular mail would continue to be sent and received via rail.

As Bush's letter to his older brother made its way to Chicago, other airmail began arriving in Amarillo.

"In some instances," the newspaper said on October 26, "letters mailed in Los Angeles Saturday morning and bearing special delivery stamps were read by Amarilloans within a few minutes of their arrival here at 3:55 o'clock Saturday afternoon."

Three days after getting the letter from his brother, William replied.

Realizing he was writing for posterity, the seventy-one-year-old businessman recalled his first trip to the Panhandle in June 1881. Traveling with his father-in-law, barbed-wire manufacturer Joseph F. Glidden, he had taken a two-day train ride from Chicago to Las Vegas in New Mexico Territory. The two men tried all day, without luck, to find someone willing to take them by buggy to the newly formed Frying Pan Ranch in Potter County, the future site of Amarillo. Finally, they got the name of someone in Springer, New Mexico, a community about fifty miles north of Las Vegas, who could take them to the ranch in Texas.

"We went there and remained over night, then started early the next morning, and we were five days and four nights where we slept in the open with horse collars for pillows, and eating 'chow' with the exception of the second day, [when] Mr. Glidden's partner shot a jackrabbit," William wrote.

Bush collected dried cow manure, which he called "prairie chips," and built a fire to cook the rabbit. After eating, they rolled on to Tascosa, where they spent the night.

"Our foreman came for us the next morning," he continued, "[and] drove us to Tecovas Springs headquarters, about 25 miles."

William Bush concluded, "It is wonderful the changes that have been made since the year 1881."

Long Road to Hamblen Drive

The designation on the official state highway map is State Highway (SH) 207, but south of Claude in Armstrong County that stretch of pavement is far better known as Hamblen Drive.

SH 207 runs for 199.7 miles from the Texas-Oklahoma border to Post. In the process, the highway cuts through Palo Duro Canyon and crosses the Prairie Dog Town Fork of the Red River. That segment, one of the most scenic drives in Texas, honors Will H. Hamblen, a onetime Armstrong County elected official who spent much of his life pushing for the roadway.

Born in 1876, Hamblen came to the Panhandle with his family in the boxcar of an immigrant train in the late fall of 1890. They built a dugout on the south rim of Palo Duro, but the small shelter didn't have enough room for everyone, so Hamblen slept in their wagon until they could build a larger residence.

As a boy, Hamblen helped his father cut cedar posts in Palo Duro and haul them to Amarillo to sell for three cents each. When they first started making the trip, they followed an old Indian trail—used by buffalo before the Indians came—across and then up the side of the rugged canyon. It was a long, tough trip. The only alternative was to bypass the canyon via the new town of Canyon.

The Hamblen Drive historical marker at a roadside park on State Highway 207. *Photo courtesy of Cindy Wallace.*

Hamblen Drive cuts across the rugged eastern side of the Palo Duro Canyon. *Photo courtesy of Cindy Wallace.*

Hamblen and his father removed rocks and did whatever else they could by hand and plow to improve the route across the canyon toward Claude. Their efforts benefited from state law, which provided that once a year a county's eligible men had to put in a few days working to maintain and improve roads passing through their property. If the landowners didn't want to help that way, they could pay a road tax.

By the time Hamblen had married and settled on a section of land on the rim of Palo Duro near the small community of Wayside, he rankled at how long it took to get to the county seat at Claude. Going to the courthouse via the Canyon–Amarillo route amounted to a 120-mile trip. The only alternative was the still-rough route across and up the side of the canyon.

Elected as Precinct 2 county commissioner in 1928, Hamblen quickly got improvements underway on the cross-canyon road he and his father had begun nearly forty years earlier. Men with picks and shovels working alongside men operating mule-drawn slips, Fresnoes and wheel scrapers removed rough spots and lessened steep grades. Two years later, Hamblen's colleagues on the court voted to name the road in his honor.

While better than it had ever been, the road still offered a rough ride across the canyon, especially the stretches going up and down its steep, rocky sides. Following congressional passage of the Public Works Administration Act in 1933, Hamblen secured federal funds to pay men a dollar a day to further improve Hamblen Drive.

Showing up for work in Hamblen's Model A truck and another farmer's Model T, the men used dynamite, hand tools and mule teams to move boulders and tame cliffs as the road became increasingly easier to navigate. But one hill stood in the way. When the road crew working up from the south met the hands assigned to the north crew, they couldn't agree on what side of the hill to go around. Finally, the foreman, a man named Bulliers, said he would turn his horse loose and see which route he chose. And that's the way the road went.

With completion of the road, though it remained unpaved, the public had its first easy access to Palo Duro. Meanwhile, on the western side of the canyon, Civilian Conservation Corps men were blasting a new road providing a drivable way down into what would become Palo Duro Canyon State Park.

On the morning of November 24, 1952, a snowy day, Hamblen left his house and walked to the post office. There he picked up a letter concerning a traffic accident he had been in earlier that month and headed across the street to talk to his insurance agent. But before he could get there, he slipped and fell on a patch of ice, suffering a fractured skull. He died eight days afterward, seventy-six years old.

Two years later, the Highway Department took over maintenance of Hamblen's road and converted it to Farm-to-Market (FM) Road 284. In addition to paving it and adding other improvements, the department built a 975-foot concrete bridge across the Prairie Dog Town Fork.

Having the road under state maintenance amounted to a tremendous improvement, but civic leaders in the Hutchinson County oil town of Borger—and others in the Panhandle—wanted a state highway connecting Borger on the north with Post on the south. But that was only a small part of the dream. The grand vision entailed a roadway that would go north from Borger via Kansas and Nebraska all the way to Canada and south beyond Post to San Angelo and Del Rio.

A year after Hamblen's death, Plainview newspaper publisher and attorney Marshall Formby gained appointment to the state highway commission. While it probably would have happened sooner or later, Formby pushed for the Panhandle segment of the proposed Canada–Mexico highway.

Accordingly, in 1958, Formby and his fellow commissioners approved the designation of FM 284 as a segment of SH 207. But the change would involve more than nomenclature. The FM's gradient, which ranged from 8.0 to 9.0 percent, would be reduced to the department's standard for highways: 6.5 percent. The new highway was dedicated on May 28 of that year.

A decade after Hamblen Drive became part of SH 207, the state put up a historical marker chronicling the route's history in 103 words. The marker stands eight miles northeast of Wayside at a roadside park overlooking Palo Duro Canyon, at a point where Hamblen's road seems to go on forever.

About the Author

M ike Cox's family tree has deep Texas roots. He began his full-time newspaper career as a reporter for the *San Angelo Standard-Times* in 1967 and later worked for the *Lubbock Avalanche-Journal* and *Austin American-Statesman*. After a twenty-year career in journalism, he joined the Texas Department of Public Safety and served as its spokesman for fifteen years. He retired from the state in 2007, but in 2010 he retired from retirement and now works in the communications division of the Texas Parks and Wildlife Department. An elected member of the Texas Institute of Letters, he is the author of twenty nonfiction books. In 2010, he received the West Texas Book and Music Festival's A.C. Greene Award for lifetime achievement. He and his wife, Linda, and their daughter, Hallie, live in Austin, Texas.

Visit us at
www.historypress.net